PENCILS OUT! Volume 4

Pointed Commentaries and Assorted Entertainments

Contents

A Commentary on *Landscape into Art* by Sir Kenneth Clark

The real title of Sir Kenneth's book should be something like *The History of Landscape as A Subject for Painters from Antiquity to the 20th Century* which the publisher may have just thought too long. *Landscape into Art* is a catchy set of words, but, like occasional parts of the book's content, it reads like something badly translated from a foreign language - like "facts become art through love."

The chapters are based on his lectures as Slade Professor, the purpose of which was to "make our English youth care somewhat for the arts," as John Ruskin, one of the professorship's founders, put it. Sir Kenneth goes on to say that he chose landscape painting because it was the chief artistic creation of the 19th century, and without an understanding of it "no evaluation of contemporary painting," which he says is the kind of art which interests young people, "is possible." However, it's really hard to see how the landscape painting of the 19th century helps "our English youth," or anyone else, to understand "contemporary painting." The book was published in 1949, the heyday of Picasso and Pollock! He says that anyone who expects the book to be "a treatise on the history of landscape painting will be disappointed," but that's exactly what it is - which doesn't mean you won't be disappointed anyway.

He more or less begins his de facto history with the claim that "the Hellenistic painter . . . evolved a school of landscape painting," but only " the Odysseus Series in the Vatican suggests that landscape had become a means of poetical expression." The trouble with this claim is that these pictures were painted in Rome c. 50 B.C. and so are *not* Hellenistic. He doesn't really talk specifically about Roman painting but there are some examples from Pompeii and

Herculaneum which can be called landscapes, as can the garden wall paintings from the Villa of Augustus's wife Livia now in the Rome Palazzo Massimo (fig 1). I'll just mention here before I go farther that I do not believe an edition of his book with good color pictures has yet been published, and the ones in my 1972 edition are bad even for black and white. There are some color pictures in this essay, but you can, of course, get good pictures of virtually everything he discusses online.

It's true that there was a long period, essentially the Middle Ages, through which landscape was not a common subject, but there are very few paintings from this long period surviving with secular subjects of any kind at all; it's not just landscape that's missing. Toward the end of the Middle Ages representations of the natural world became more common, as in the frescoes of the Campo Santo in Pisa, and Clark says that the first landscapes "in the modern sense" are in Ambrogio Lorenzetti's 14th century frescoes in the Siena Palazzo Pubblico (1338-1339) (fig. 2), although a couple of pages later he says that the *Turin Hours Book* has the "first modern landscapes".

He also says that "for the first time since antiquity the pursuits of country life are represented as a source of happiness and poetry" in the picture Simone Martini made (1336) for the frontispiece of Petrarch's copy of Virgil's Eclogues and Georgics (fig. 3). Further, the paintings in the Tour de la Garde Robe in the Papal Palace at Avignon (1343) are "the first complete examples of the landscape of symbols," and they exhibit "an untroubled enjoyment of open air life"(fig. 4). I don't know what he means by a "landscape of symbols" but the open air life part is obvious.

He says that in 1425 Hubert Van Eyck painted the "first great modern landscape," in the center of the Ghent Altarpiece (figure 5), the above examples not, I guess, being "great." One problem with this claim is that almost no one now gives Hubert Van Eyck sole credit for this altarpiece; at best he is said to have, in some sense, begun it, and his brother Jan is said to have finished it in 1432, 6 years after Hubert's death. It is, in fact, now not considered certain that *any* surviving picture is wholly by Hubert, and the *Britannica* says that the inscription from the frame which only survives in what is thought to be a copy, and which says that Hubert began it and Jan finished it, is "wholly questionable."

Although it's not unlikely that this picture contains images of actual buildings, e.g., perhaps the Cathedral of Utrecht to the left of center, he says that the first indisputable piece of topography - actual landscape - is in the *Miraculous Draught of Fishes* by Konrad Witz (1444); he says it depicts the shore of Lake Geneva. I guess, but the landscapes in the *Très*

Riches Heures of Jean de Berry, e.g., figure 7 (c. 1415), according to Clark, are rendered with an "objectivity" surpassed only by Pieter Bruegel (whose name he misspells). Figure 7 is the October page with the Louvre across the Seine; it was painted about 30 years before Witz's picture, which is, it's true, actually much larger at least - about 5' wide.

He says that Dürer's watercolor of Innsbruck (fig. 8) "is the first portrait of a town," (c. 1495) although he painted a "portrait" of Nuremberg about the same time, and that he painted the first "sentimental" landscapes of "modern painting," e.g., the fisherman's house in figure 9. It should also be noticed that these are "pure" landscapes not including any human activity.

He says Pollaiuolo's *Rape of Dejaniera* (c. 1470) (fig. 10) is the first picture in which landscape is essential, not incidental, but I'd certainly say it's pretty essential in at least some of the *Très Riches Heures* pictures.

He says that the most beautiful landscapes of the 1460's are the ones on the reverse of the double portrait of Federigo da Montefeltro and his wife by Piero della Francesca. Figure 11 is the one on the back of the portrait of Federigo.

However, I do think that Giovanni Bellini's *Agony in the Garden*, for one, ought to get some votes; figure 12 is a detail from it. Piero's landscape doesn't look like anything on this planet!

I've mentioned in other commentaries on his commentaries that he is prone to use the "pontifical superlative" and say things like "this is *the first* . . ." or

"this is *the most* . . ." without qualification. In talking about Bellini's *St. Francis in Ecstasy* (1475-80)(fig. 13), however, he does allow for some difference of opinion; of it he says, "No other great painting *perhaps* contains such a quantity of natural details observed and rendered with incredible patience" (my italics). Impressive as this picture is, that would be a hard claim to justify without qualification.

He also emphasizes the treatment of light in this picture quoting Sebastian Franck, the 16th century mystic, who says, in effect, that light is a manifestation of the divine presence; this is also reminiscent of what Abbot Suger de Saint-Denis

says back in the 12th century about the quality of the light passing through the stained glass windows of his church.

The *Saint Francis* wasn't painted in the 1460's but it certainly has one of the most beautiful landscapes of the century.

Sir Kenneth says that "The High Renaissance Style which dates from the first years of Raphael and Michelangelo in Rome," played down landscape and made the human body omnipotent, and it's certainly true that Michelangelo at least never painted landscapes in more than a very perfunctory way. I would point out, however, that quite a few of Raphael's pictures, even if they are dominated by human figures, do contain memorable landscapes, and he was, if anything, more influential than Michaelangelo.

Clark says Pieter Bruegel is "the one master of naturalistic landscape who comes between Bellini and the 17th century." What about Titian? He certainly painted a lot of pictures in the 16th century which aren't that different in composition, as far as landscape goes, than most of Bellini's. Figure 14 is a picture of Titian's *Madonna with the Rabbit* (1530).

Clark is a great admirer of Bruegel, and says that his pictures like *Hunters in The Snow* (1565)(fig. 15) are among "those very rare works . . . which have a widespread and immediate appeal" like, he says, Handel's *Messiah* and *Pilgrim's Progress*. That's a strange pairing though; I bet everyone reading this has heard Handel's *Messiah*, and *no* one reading this has read *Pilgrim's Progress*. Anyway, *Hunters in The Snow* is a very impressive painting.

Clark says that "the landscape of fact" is "a bourgeois form of art" and 17th century Holland was the great epoch of this. Nevertheless, he claims that the Dutch let Rembrandt go bankrupt and let Ruisdael starve. It's certainly misleading to say that the Dutch "let" Rembrandt go bankrupt - he made a fortune which he spent on a mansion and who knows what else. Ruisdael didn't starve; his paintings sold for twice what most other painters got, and the myth that he died in the poorhouse was

disproven well before Clark made this claim - and Clark also misspells his name; the spelling he uses, Ruysdael, is the one used by his uncle Salomon, also an important painter. Anyway, he says that he was "the greatest master of the natural vision before Constable," whatever *that* means, but I do think he's as great a painter as Constable (whatever *that* means). The picture by Ruisdael which Clark includes he calls *A View near Haarlem* (c. 1660)(fig. 16).

Vermeer is now considered one of the very greatest Dutch painters, and, although he rarely painted landscapes, his *View of Delft* (c. 1660)(fig. 17) is always considered one of the most impressive ever painted, and I suppose Clark means to be in agreement with this when he says that it is "certainly the nearest which painting has ever come to a colored photograph." It certainly looks "realistic" but I don't think it looks like a photograph. For one thing, the shadows seem to indicate the sun should be in the distance, not, as it were, behind the viewer where it seems to be; it's shining brightly on the roofs of the buildings in the distance in the middle of the picture, and the human figures cast no shadows at all. Actually I think the picture looks more like a photograph in a photograph than it does when you see it in person.

There are many other pictures which look more like photographs than this does, e.g., some of the portraits by, or after, Frans Pourbus the Younger, like the one in figure 18 of Albert Archduke of Austria (c. 1615 or later). Actually it is often *not* thought a compliment if a picture by a 17th century painter is said to look like a photograph anyway - and certainly Frans Pourbus the Younger, let alone the anonymous copyist if that's who really painted the portrait, is never put at the same level as Vermeer for all his ability to produce a photo-like picture.

Canaletto's pictures often remind people of photos, and he has always been one of my favorite painters because I like seeing what things looked like hundreds of years ago. Clark doesn't like some of his pictures just because they were made for English clients, but most painters certainly did consider what their clients wanted! Figure 19 is Canaletto's view of the west end of the Grand canal in Venice.

In addition to the "landscape of fact" which we see illustrated in the pictures by Ruisdael, Vermeer, and Canaletto, there is also the "landscape of fantasy" which, although there are earlier examples, Sir Kenneth thinks is best represented by the work of Grünewald and Altdorfer; in fact he calls the Isenheim altarpiece (c. 1514) by Grünewald ``perhaps the most phenomenal picture ever painted," but it isn't a "picture" it's a whole altarpiece with *lots* of pictures, including *The Torment of Saint Anthony* (fig. 20) which he says is "near to the vulgarity which accompanies toomuchness." He even says that only "a distinction of color and style prevents a comparison with Walt Disney." I'd call that a phenomenal comparison. I do agree, however, that there is something almost cartoonish about the saint's tormentors.

He says that the world into which St. Paul the Hermit (he's the figure on the right talking to St. Anthony, in figure 21) has retreated, is of a desolation "never again attempted in painting," but I think some of Caspar David Friedrich's pictures,

e.g., *The Abbey in The Oakwood* (1810)(fig.22), are pretty good attempts at this.

He calls Piero di Cosimo's *Forest Fire* (c. 1500) (fig. 23) the first picture by an Italian in which man is of no consequence,

but there is at least Leonardo's "View of the Arno" which pre-dates Piero's picture by several decades and, unlike the latter, has no men in it at all - although it is true it's not a finished painting. Piero's strange picture which seems to show animals escaping from a not very threatening fire is consistent with the eccentric character Vasari attributes to him.

Another example of the landscape of fantasy is Altdorfer's *Battle of Alexander* (1529)(fig.24) which Clark calls "the supreme manifestation of untameable nature."

He says that the work of Joachim Patinir constitutes "the first series of pure landscapes." Usually art historians refer to a "pure landscape" as one with no human figures, or at least very insignificant ones not involved in some important

event, but Patinir's pictures usually have some people in them, and in the one Clark picks to show us, *Charon Crossing the Styx* (c. 1520) (fig. 25), Charon, although he's human only in appearance here, is an important part of the picture, and he's right in the center of it. The landscape dominates the picture, but some would not call it a *pure* landscape.

One of the strangest things Clark says is that Hieronymous Bosch was a big influence on Giorgione! It's hard to think of two painters whose typical pictures are apparently more different.

The two examples he shows are, first of all, just landscapes in the largest sense. One picture which he says is a "Giorgione design" which survives only in an engraving by Marc Antonio called "Raphael's Dream" is not attributed to Giorgione by the National Gallery or the British Museum which own copies of the engraving. It's apparently called "Raphael's Dream" because it was once attributed to Raphael. Clark himself doesn't say why he thinks it's a

Giorgione. The little monsters approaching the women do, at least, remind one of Bosch, whoever was responsible for the picture (fig. 26)

Clark also attributes the picture which he calls the *Shipwreck* (c. 1505?) (fig. 27) to Giorgione, but no one else does; it's been attributed to Palma Vecchio since Vasari wrote his biography. It is a very strange picture which does, as Clark suggests, look almost like it's been put together from pieces of various other paintings. I think it could be called "Palma Vecchio's Dream."

Thinking then that it's Giorgione's work, Clark says "we are dumbfounded by the power of genius for here is a work which . . . points directly to Gericault and Turner." No comment.

Clark calls Rubens "one of the greatest of all landscape painters" which is not an honor he is usually given, partly at least because he doesn't paint many not dominated by some human activity. The *Philemon and Baucis* which he discusses

does include human actors, but it's true that they are incidental compared to the impressive landscape which wholly dominates the picture (fig. 28).

In the chapter called "Ideal Landscape" he

discusses Giorgione's *Tempest* (c. 1507) (fig. 29); he says "it's one of those works of art before which the scholar had best remain silent," and then he talks more about it than almost any other picture in the book. He says Giorgione's *Sleeping Venus* (not shown) "must have been one of the most beautiful pictures in the world before it was damaged and restored" but Giorgione's part in it, if any, is now thought uncertain, and Titian is usually said to be the artist who should get most of the credit for it - at least for the landscape which is supposed to be the subject of interest in Clark's discussions.

Clark is an admirer of both Claude Lorrain and Nicholas Poussin; he calls the former's *Acis and Galatea* (1657)(fig.30) one of his greatest "poems." He says Claude's work is "gentle and inarticulate" while Poussin's is "stern and Cartesian."

I think what I'd say is that a lot of what each does *can* be described as "lyrical" it's just that their styles are different. Maybe that's what Clark means.

He says that Poussin didn't paint any pure landscapes until about 1648, but, again, it depends on what you call a "pure landscape." I think Poussin painted no pictures at all without human figures; he painted no bare stages without actors. Clark uses Poussin's *St. John on Patmos* (fig. 31), probably his most well known picture, to illustrate how he gives "logical form to the disorder of natural scenery," and he makes another - I'd say "jaw dropping" claim although I don't like that expression - when he says that "without some knowledge of (Poussin's landscapes) we cannot understand Cezanne and Seurat." Derek Hill in *Spectator* says "no living writer on art could have treated his subject with greater clarity than Sir Kenneth Clark." It's hard to believe he actually read what Sir Kenneth says about comparing Poussin to Seurat.

Clark says that Poussin's brother-in-law, Gaspard Dughet, is "one of the most underrated artists in the history of painting." The picture he shows to illustrate this claim is *A Road near Albano* (c. 1670) (fig. 32). I wouldn't really argue about this;

I've written in earlier volumes about how impressive a lot of paintings by little-known artists are.

A pretty much forgotten 19th century English painter, Samuel Palmer, is a landscape painter whom Clark likes, and who does some pure landscapes, although most of his pictures include very small people playing insignificant roles. Figure 33 is an example of his work called *Wilmot's Hill* (c. 1851); this is essentially a watercolor, but he painted in a lot of different media in a lot of different styles. "No less than Wordsworth,"

Clark says, "Palmer invested nature with a spiritual quality."

"However," says Clark, "it was the genius of Constable which first discovered . . . the art of unquestioning naturalism," and he also succeeded "in subordinating the visual data of landscape to a single pictorial idea." He says, *The Willows by a Stream* (c. 1830) (fig. 34) shows "the most complete acceptance of all the facts of vision which has ever been made in art," but then he says his finished pictures are boring! A genius shouldn't produce boring pictures.

Constable was a great admirer of Poussin but, apart from the obvious difference in style - you'd never mistake a landscape by one for a work by the other - Poussin's almost always are inspired by some classical or Biblical subject, and Constable's, I think, never are. The people in Constable's pictures are ordinary, not heroes or saints. Constable said "I never saw an ugly thing in my life," which is close to the claim that a great artist can make a masterpiece out of anything. It's a little

disingenuous though - he never painted anything most people would call ugly.

Surprisingly, Clark doesn't spend much time on the Barbizon School which was pretty much wholly devoted to landscape painting; Theodore Rousseau is the only one of that group to get much attention. Clark uses the picture which he calls *A Summer Day* and which the Louvre calls *The Oaks of Apremont* (c. 1851) (fig. 35) to illustrate Rousseau's style which Clark calls "static" whereas Constable's is "dynamic" whatever that means. *A Summer Day* does look a little more windblown, but I don't think most of Constable's pictures do.

Clark seems to prefer Corot, who did spend some time at Barbizon, to Rousseau because the latter lacked Corot's "unselfconscious abandonment to nature." But then he says his tastes "were entirely classic," and he admired Poussin, which sounds like a contradiction! People who do art historical commentary sometimes just seem to make up their own rules about what makes sense and what doesn't. He says that the Louvre version of the *Bridge at Narni* (1826) (fig. 36) "is as free as the most vigorous Constable," but the version in the Canadian National Gallery (1827) (fig. 37) is "tamer than the tamest imitation of Claude (Lorraine)." Since he doesn't even put bad black and white pictures of them in the book, you can compare them here.

In the Louvre version the bridge is more monumental - it dominates the picture more - but does it look "free"? I *would* at least say the treatment of the landscape is perhaps more "free," especially

the part to the left of the river. Maybe by including peasants in the second version Corot was intending to make some sort of point about the difference between then and now; their insignificant sheep herding over against the reminder of the greatness of Roman achievement, for he was certainly an admirer of the latter.

Clark says that when Corot began painting "nymphs dancing among feathery trees" this increased his popularity "disastrously," but then he says that some of these are "extremely beautiful," and that *The Souvenir of Mortefontaine* (1864), probably his most popular painting, is a masterpiece! He doesn't give you a picture of it, so I will (fig. 38). The figures aren't very nymph-like, but the trees are "feathery," in fact not very many figures in any of his landscapes are really ones I'd call "nymphs."

Gustave Courbet's landscapes are rarely considered his most important pictures, but Clark says he put up 14 in his 1855 show. However, the example he gives us, *Cliffs at Étretat* (fig. 39), wasn't painted until 1869, so I'm not sure what he says about it is useful. Anway, he does say "it anticipates in an incomprehensible way the colored postcard." Since his picture is *not* colored, you

can see if mine looks like a colored postcard "in an incomprehensible way."

Clark says the landscapes which Charles-François Daubigny exhibited at the Salon were popular "and that is exactly what is wrong with them." His example is what he calls "The Quarry" (fig. 40) and the Louvre calls *The Flood-gate at Optevoz*. This seems to be an example of the sort of art-historical snobbery of which Sir Kenneth has sometimes been accused. Popular art is bad art. But, really, what's more popular than the Mona Lisa? The Sistine Chapel ceiling? I suppose his point is that an artist who paints

something that's popular is discouraged from perhaps creating something more "worthy" in some sense, but I think this would be hard to document.

Clark says that the Monet, Sisley, and Pissarro pictures painted during the 1860's to 1874 "achieved the most complete naturalism which has ever been made into art." He compares Pissarro's *Norwood* (1870) (fig.41) to. B.W. Leader's

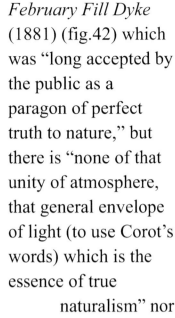

February Fill Dyke (1881) (fig.42) which was "long accepted by the public as a paragon of perfect truth to nature," but there is "none of that unity of atmosphere, that general envelope of light (to use Corot's words) which is the essence of true naturalism" nor is there "unity of any kind" in Leader's picture. So what; I like Leader's as much - and you could have more or less 20 by him for what one by the more fashionable Pissarro would cost today.

He refers to Sisley's picture of "Hampton Court" but he painted several and none are included in the book, so that makes it hard to understand how the picture, whatever he has in mind, was "the perfect moment of Impression." Anyway, on the next page he says that Impressionism was born in 1869 when Renoir and Monet "began to work on the same motive" which he implies was the reflection of light on water at La Grenouillere, a riverside gathering place on the edge of Paris. He

doesn't show the pictures they painted there, so you can see them here. Figure 43 is Monet's version and figure 44 is Renoir's. Manet called Monet "the Raphael of water!"

Clark devotes almost as much time to J. M. W. Turner as he does to anyone else, except maybe Cezanne. It's difficult to generalize about his style because he painted some pictures that are straightforward images of easily recognizable things and others are very dream - or nightmare - like. Clark refers to his picture with the complicated title *Light and Color (Goethe's Theory) - the Morning After the Deluge - Moses Writing the Book of Genesis* (c. 1843) (fig. 45), but the illustration, 85 in *his* book, is a picture of *The Evening of the Deluge*, not that there's a lot

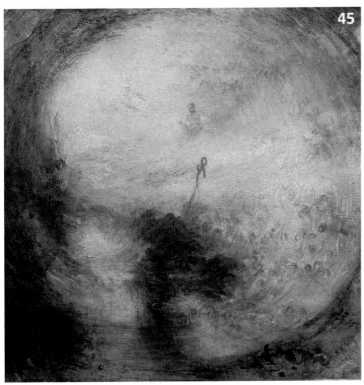

of difference; they both look as though they could have been painted at Los Alamos after a nuclear test.

To me the most impressive of Turner's pictures has always been *The Fighting Temeraire tugged to her last birth to be broken up* (1836) (fig. 46). Like a lot of pictures, it's painted in a language that is easy enough to read but hard to translate.

Clark does mention impressionism in connection with Turner, and it is true that some of the language used to describe his work is often used to describe the work of the impressionists. Monet and Pissarro saw his work in London while they were there during the Franco-Prussian War. John Rewald in *The History of Impressionism* quotes Pissarro on Turner: "The paintings of Turner and Constable, the canvases of Old Crome, have certainly had influence upon us . . ." but "while they taught us something, showed us that they had no understanding of the analysis of shadow . . ." Monet commented to a friend that Turner's work was "antipathetic to him because of the exuberant romanticism of his fancy." "Old Crome" incidentally is John Crome, another underrated painter not even mentioned by Clark. His pictures usually sell for a few thousand dollars at auction.

I don't think many, if any, pictures by Monet or Pissarro would be confused with Turner's work, but the emphasis on light and color rather than form is, at least, something which they have in common with him.

Clark says that Monet undertook to prove "that the painted object was of no importance, the sensation of light was the only true subject." To prove this he famously chose to paint a cathedral facade and a bunch of haystacks and Clark doesn't like the results - "disastrous" is his word, and they are hard to like.

A lot of what he says about impressionism is, not surprisingly, hard to understand. He says "What pleasures could be … more eternal than those portrayed in Renoir's *Déjeuner des Canotiers*; what images of an earthly paradise more persuasive than the white sails in Monet's estuaries?" However then he says that "the supreme creation of art is the compelling image," but that impressionism aimed at abolishing images!

Clark says that it's appropriate that Seurat's *Sunday Afternoon on the Grande Jatte* (1884-86) (figure 47) was the chief exhibit at the last impressionist exhibition " for nothing could mark more clearly the end of impressionist doctrines." He admits that "even after long familiarity with the original I still find the Grande Jatte a disconcerting work." He was only 21 when it came to Chicago in 1924 so I'm not sure what he means by familiarity with "the original." Did he ever actually see it at all? Again there's no picture of it in the book but you can see it in mine. One thing that always amazes me about it is how big it is - 10' wide - and how much work went into making it!

The idea, more or less, was that rather than the painter mixing the colors, the pointillist technique, as it was called, would require the eye itself to do that. It's been compared to the way the pixels on your computer screen work, only Seurat's "pixels" are *way* too big to produce the effect he wanted.

Clark doesn't spend much time on Van Gogh, and I think he exaggerates his madness. It's true that after the ear mutilation he could be described as at least very unstable, but up to the last year or so of his life, at least, it doesn't seem reasonable to call him insane. Of the hundreds of surviving letters he wrote, very few suggest the author was crazy. Clark actually thinks that because his pictures look like the work of a madman, that helped make them popular! Turner's Deluge pictures look more like the work of a madman than anything Van Gogh painted. Clark says that Van Gogh and Gauguin "destroyed" impressionism, but a lot of what he says about the work of, e.g., Monet could be said about many of Van Gogh's paintings - or Gauguin's. His language is often so imprecise it would be no help in telling the work of one painter from that of another. Whose pictures "enlarged our range of vision"? What styles "expressed a real and valuable ethical position"? Which artist would you say "recaptured the light key?" etc. Look at his black and white pictures and see if you can find the answers. He's trying to translate one artform into another, and he might as well try playing something on a piano.

He spends a lot of time on Cezanne, perhaps because he was the painter who seems to have most interested him at the start of his career. He says that his painting of "orgies" shows that his genius was "based on a colossal sensuality," but there's a difference between an orgy and simple nude sunbathing. He complains about Turner's inability to paint the human figure and says that many are "remarkably ugly" and his figure of Napoleon is "pathetically ill-drawn," but not many painted nudes are uglier than a lot of Cezanne's. He says the latter's first important landscape is *The Cutting* (c. 1870) (Fig. 48) with "a stunning boldness," and "largeness of vision," and "frontality of attack." O.K.

His many pictures of Mont Sainte-Victoire, e.g., figure 49, c. 1887, remind me a little of Monet's pictures of the Cathedral of Rouen and the haystacks, although the purpose in Cezanne's case wasn't specifically to just paint the effects of light. His friend Joachim Gasquet wrote a book about him in which he says Cezanne told him he wanted to give the mountain a kind of cosmic significance. It's a little surprising that Clark doesn't pay much attention to these pictures.

The Epilogue contains some of Clark's most obscure language. He says what he wants to call "museum art" implies "the existence of the pure aesthetic sensation." This sounds like something Clive Bell, whose positive review of the book is on the cover, would say - it's just the appearance of the work that counts (I've argued against this elsewhere).

Clark says that we find this "pure aesthetic essence" in its "purest and most concentrated form in the early Middle Ages or in the work of primitive peoples." He thinks that the first artist to state that he was directly aiming at this was Gauguin and his Tahitian landscapes "are true successors to the tapestry landscapes of the 14th century." But 14th century tapestries don't represent either the early Middle Ages or the work of primitive people. The picture Clark shows us to support this claim is another mistake - it's a picture by Henri Rousseau (figure 103 in the book). The right picture is apparently figure 102, called *Paysage avec Cochons noirs* but I've never seen this picture attributed to Gauguin in any other source. He also says the Louvre has two of Rousseau's greatest paintings, but doesn't include pictures or even tell us what they are!

He closes with an attempt to put abstract art in an historical context and to this end he quotes Alfred Barr, the first Director of the Museum of Modern Art and Plato! Barr says "Since resemblance to nature is at best superfluous and at worst distracting, it might as well be eliminated." Plato talks about the beauty of pure shapes and colors. But with regard to what Plato says, a lot of abstract art is not meant to be "beautiful." Of course a lot of things in the whole history of art do not strike one as beautiful either; if I had to choose the word I would associate with art that interests me it might be "impressive" - impressive because it *is* beautiful like landscapes by Corot or Constable *inter alia*, or historically interesting like the ceiling of Saint- Savin sur Gartempe, or an amazing technical achievement like the Ghent Altarpiece. The banana that the Guggenheim let Maurizio Catalan tape to an exhibit wall was eaten by someone, so maybe we will have to add that an important work of art can be edible. Richard Armstrong is the Director of the Guggenheim who thought the banana was worth displaying - remember that name.

Close encounters of the First Kind

This is just a quick look at some of the first, or at least early and interesting, accounts in which Europeans have reported their discoveries in other parts of the world.

Herodotus (c. 484-425 B.C.) is someone who perhaps ought to be thought of not only as "the Father of History," primarily because of his treatment of the war between Greece and Persia, but as the first famous "tourist" in something like the modern sense. Most of the places to which he traveled beyond Europe had already been visited for one reason or another by many before him - he was not an "explorer" as that word is usually used now - but he is the first European to write about some of these places in an interesting way. One such place is Egypt where he spent at least several months during which he traveled up the Nile as far as Elephantine, just short of the location of the modern Aswan Dam. He was curious, for example, about what the source of the Nile might be, and about what caused the yearly rise and fall of the river level, so important to Egyptian agriculture - and Egyptian life in general. In fact no one could give him an acceptable account of where the source might be, and he thought the theory he was given that melting snow to the far south caused the river to rise in the spring was ridiculous, since all he could see was hot desert. In fact, the source of the White Nile, the longer section of the river, wasn't to be established until the 19th c., and with regard to the melting snow theory, it's now known that it is part of the reason for the river's rise, although seasonal rainfall, also well south of Elephantine of course, is now said to be a bigger factor.

He goes into considerable, and interesting, length describing the sometimes bizarre customs and what can I guess be called at least the nominally religious practices of people he encountered, e.g., how if a cat dies in a house, all the members of the family shave their eyebrows, but if a dog dies everyone shaves his or her head and whole body! He says that in parts of Egypt crocodiles are regarded as sacred and some are picked out and treated as pampered pets, while at Elephantine they are regarded as enemies and eaten whenever they are caught.

One of the most important parts of what he has to say about his trip to Egypt concerns the Great Pyramid, and, amazingly, his reference to it is the earliest to survive, 2000 years after it was built. I've talked about this in the book *From The Pyramids to*

Pompeii and in the YouTube video *Ancient Civilization Lecture 2A*, but if you haven't taken advantage of those, he says he was told that it took 100,000 slaves 20 years to build it. Modern authorities think the time frame is perhaps about right, but that a smaller workforce was involved, probably not made up of slaves, but of men who, according to the most sanguine supposition, may have gotten some satisfaction out of their part in the end result - according to the trickle down theory of glory. He was also told that the then still surviving inscriptions on the casing stones were lists of what the workers were fed, which seems incredible, and that one of the smaller pyramids was built for Pharaoh's daughter who required a stone for it from each of her lovers and it probably has 10,000 stones in it!

Herodotus did not visit India, but he does devote a few pages to some of the things he's heard about what it's like, including a report of strange cannibalistic practices and an account of the giant gold mining ants that were said to live there - one of the weirder stories about ancient India to survive!

Flavius Arrianus (c. 86-160 A.D.), known as Arrian, is most famous for his *Anabasis*, his account of the 4th c. B.C. adventure which took Alexander the Great to India and back. Ptolemy, one of Alexander's generals who later established the Ptolemaic dynasty in Egypt, wrote an eyewitness report which was Arrian's main source, but it does not survive. In the *Anabasis* Arrian says he doesn't talk much about Indian customs, way of life, etc, because he is going to write another book *Indica* which will cover this sort of thing - and he did. For this book he relied primarily on the now mostly lost works of Alexander's Fleet commander, Nearchus (c. 360-300 B.C.), and Megasthenes (350-290 B.C.) who is usually considered the first European to have left a written description of India based on his own experience, but as you can see they are essentially contemporary.

In the *Indica* Arrian refers quite a bit to what Nearchus and Megasthenes have to say about all the strange animals to be found in India - elephants, tigers, and, interestingly, the gold mining ants again! According to Arrian, Nearchus says he never saw one, but did see their skins! Megasthenes, says Arrian, just quoted hearsay, and then he says "Since I have no certainty . . ., I readily dismiss this subject of ants." He also reports that Nearchus describes how miraculous it seems that parrots can speak with a human voice.

With regard to elephants, one interesting thing Arrian says, although he doesn't refer to a source, is that "Their women, such as are of great modesty, can be seduced by no other gift, but yield themselves to anyone who gives an elephant; and the Indians think it no disgrace to yield thus on the gift of an elephant, but rather it seems honorable for a woman that her beauty should be valued at an elephant."

Arrian also devotes a lot of time to the account Nearchus gave of his return to the west via the sea while Alexander was returning by land, and he refers to the sighting of whales, and says that when they spouted, it startled the sailors so much they dropped their oars.

These are the sorts of things which stick in the minds of most of us who are casual readers, but Arrian also does discuss quite a lot of more important (I guess) sociological material, the sources for which are, again, Nearchus and Megasthenes. For example, he talks about the caste system, says that in India there are no slaves, and that the people are typically thin and tall.

Pytheas of Marseille (c. 350-300 B.C.) is the first to write about Britain; however, as with the accounts of Nearchus and Megasthenes, we only have access to his work through references made to it by later writers since the original text is lost. He may have sailed all the way around the British Isles, but there is some doubt about this; he apparently did at least get as far north as the Orkney Islands.

According to Strabo (c. 63 B.C.- 25 A.D.) Pytheas refers to Britain as *Britannikē*. This name is derived from the Welsh Pry-dein = Bri-tain. "Pryd" means "form" or "picture" in Welsh, so the people of Britain were the "picture" or "painted" people, i.e., "Picts," because, apparently, of the popularity of tattooing among them. According to Pytheas they lived simply in thatched huts, ate primarily bread, and relied on chariots in warfare.

Pytheas is also usually said to have left a written account of the Baltic Sea, having gone at least as far as the mouth of the Vistula River.

The visit of Pytheas to Britain was primarily in the form of a voyage along the coast, and the first at all extensive account of the land is in the *De Bello Gallico* of Julius Caesar. Caesar's first army of invasion consisted of a relatively small force of 2 legions which probably landed in Pegwell Bay about 10 miles east of Canterbury. They had a rough time of it, and Caesar also mentions the skillful use of chariots by the Britons. Weather was also a big problem, and high tides inflicted a lot of damage on his ships. He had not landed until late August 55 B.C. and his army was in no condition to face winter there, so he was forced to leave without achieving anything, apart from the landing itself, about which he could brag. Nevertheless, he was treated as a hero when he returned to Rome.

The following year, 54 B.C., he again crossed the channel with far more ships, men, and supplies. This time he was able to advance inland probably to about where Wheathampstead is now just north of London, and he accepted there the surrender of the British chief Cassivellaunus who agreed to give over hostages and send tribute, but although Roman sovereignty was acknowledged "on paper" as it were, Caesar was again forced by the approach of winter to take his army back to Gaul.

It is in his account of the second invasion that he says a bit more about the British and their lifestyle. The population, he says, is very large and the place is thickly studded with homesteads, with the most civilized inhabitants living in the south. He says, like Pytheas 300 years earlier, that they all paint themselves - Caesar says with blue woad.. For money they use bronze and gold coins, and he says the weather is actually better than in Gaul!

According to a recent (2023) BBC documentary, there is some evidence that Europeans were in China at least as early as the 3rd c. B.C., and we know that the Italian Franciscan Giovanni da Pian del Carpine visited and wrote about Mongolia in the 1240's, but the Venetian Marco Polo is the first to *recount* his experiences in what we call China today. He was there from about 1271 to 1295. On his return he wound up imprisoned by the Genovese, Genoa being at war with Venice at the time, and, oddly, dictated his memoir, rather than wrote it himself with his own hand, to a fellow prisoner named Rustichello da Pisa who was a writer of romances and is generally thought to have somewhat embellished what Marco told him in the interest of making it a best-seller; it has even been argued, very unconvincingly according to most scholars, that Marco never went to China at all!

In brief, his father and brother had been to the court of Kublai Khan before Marco, and took him with them on a second trip. Given that *The Travels of Marco Polo* is at least an essentially accurate document, he was treated very well by Kublai Khan and his court, quickly learned several dialects, and was given important positions in the administration. Among the things that interested him were paper money, porcelain, the importance of salt, and the unfamiliar varieties of plant and animal life. He says he saw what were probably wild yaks, although he says they were almost as big as elephants, and pheasants twice the size of western ones, and lots of more familiar birds like swans and partridges. He mentions the importance of the blue stone, lapis lazuli, which was very important in early European Renaissance art and beyond.

This isn't the place to go into detail about all the various things he saw, but he was amazed by the Emperor's 10,000 white horses and some magic and jugglery performances, including one in which a man apparently had his arms and legs cut off and was then put back together! He liked the Chinese rice wine which he said makes one drunk very fast, and he was interested in the black stones they dug out of the ground which they burned and which we now call coal. Coal mining was not uncommon in Europe, even in antiquity, but Marco apparently didn't know about it.

On his return trip to Europe by sea he passed along the coast of India, but the *Mirabilia Descripta* of Jordanus, who traveled over much more of India than Marco Polo did beginning about 1321, is a much more valuable source of information, although as I've mentioned, we know of written accounts that are much earlier, e.g.,those by Ptolemy, Nearchus and Megasthenes referred to above. Jordanus became the first bishop of an Indian diocese.

We now know that there was a temporary Norse settlement on Newfoundland in the early 11th c. which represents the first known contact between Europe and the Americas, but there was no written account left. However, many years later of course, Columbus made his famous landfall somewhere in the Bahamas on an island he calls Guanahani, and which is possibly San Salvador. He is, of course, considered the discoverer of "America " with some reason, but he never set foot on any part of the United States, and believed to his dying day he had reached the Indies.

The year after his 1492 expedition he wrote an account of it in a letter to Luis de Santángel, the treasurer of Ferdinand and Isabella, who financed him, in which he says that the natives seem to have thought his ships had come from Heaven. He says, among many other interesting things, that the women work harder than the men, and the men seem satisfied with one wife, though a chief can have 20 or so. He says he encountered no monster like men, although at least one tribe was vicious and cannibalistic. He claimed that gold was plentiful, along with a lot of other things like cotton and spices.

In 1497 the Italian explorer known in England as John Cabot was likely the first European to set foot on the North American continent, or at least Newfoundland, since the Norse adventurers. A fellow named John Day who must have had contact with either Cabot himself or at least members of the expedition, wrote a letter to a Spanish official briefly describing Cabot's voyage and noting that the area where they landed was apparently inhabited, but saying little more. The Day letter also does, however, contain an allusion to the possibility that others had made a similar voyage as early as 1480.

In any case, Giovanni Verrazzano was likely the first European to set foot on what is now the United States in 1524. On his return he wrote a letter describing what he had seen to Francis I who had sponsored his voyage. He says that on one occasion his party was approached by a native with a burning stick, as though to offer them fire in a friendly gesture. They then showed him how they could make fire with gunpowder and this made the fellow tremble in terror. When they then fired off their guns, he was paralyzed!

At another stop he again met friendly natives, some of whom came aboard his ship and were understandably amazed by it. He did not go far inland, maybe 25 miles or so, and described the country as very beautiful. At another place, however, the natives were not so friendly and when the sailors ran out of trinkets to throw ashore to them, "they bared their arses at us . . . laughing uproariously the whole time."

 He says that none of the people he encountered seemed to have religious faith of any kind, did not worship idols or conduct sacrifices to pagan gods, all of which led him to think they would be easy to convert to Christianity.

And so the dikes were opened.

CAIRO WITHOUT A MAP:
A COMMENTARY ON *BAGHDAD WITHOUT A MAP* BY TONY HORWITZ

Tony Horwitz died in 2019 at just the age of 60 and, considering the sorts of adventures he recounts in this and some of his other books, he was certainly lucky to live *that* long. *Baghdad Without a Map* belongs to a sort of sub-genre of travel books which are essentially more about the personal experiences of the author and less about the historical and cultural context of the places in question - beyond a background of more or less contemporary events anyway. H.V. Morton comes to mind as someone whose books are much more devoted to placing the author's travel experiences in a larger historico-cultural framework. His book *In The Steps of St. Paul* is an example of this sort of thing. I'm not making any value judgment here - just pointing out a difference in approach. Also, neither of these books is meant to be a "guidebook" like, say, *Strolling Through Istanbul* by Hilary Sumner-Boyd and John Freely, a third sub-genre of travel writing.

Books like those of Horwitz and Morton are classified as non-fiction, but there are certainly parts of them which are reconstructions of events, based sometimes more loosely sometimes less, on what actually happened. For example, I don't think any author of books like these wrote down conversations as they were happening - as Horwitz seems to in his description of his experiences at the Arizona Bar in Cairo called "Dancing Sheik to Sheik" - a chapter title which some might think unworthy of a Pulitzer Prize winning author, but I figure this is the piece he sold to *Playboy*. Of course the line between fiction and nonfiction is often not as clear as your local library would make it seem.

Although the book is called *Baghdad Without A Map*, he talks a lot about his experiences in other parts of the Middle East including Cairo. I was in Cairo in 1988, possibly while Horwitz himself was there working on his career as a free-lance journalist, and I'm amazed by his description of it; as brave as he was, could he ever have been brave enough to go back after this book was published? Among other things he says that "it was the most awful and bewildering place my jet lagged eyes had ever beheld." He says that between his hotel and the Egyptian museum "lay a dense moat of flesh and combustion swirling dizzily through the gloom." I guess this was his first experience in a third world country, but he must have realized it wouldn't be quite like Fort Wayne, Indiana where he'd begun his career.

He says there were buses so overloaded "that bodies draped from the doors, limbs stuck out of windows and a few brave passengers even clung to the rooftops , their turbans unraveling in the wind."

Figure 1 is a picture I took of a street scene in Cairo that just happened to have a bus in it with no projecting limbs or unraveling turbans. I took the picture because the fellow in the center had the largest turban in the city.

He says the air was a "greasy malodorous broth of dust, dirt, donkey dung, and carbon monoxide." Figure 2 is the minaret of the Al Azhar Mosque in the center of Cairo against a clear blue sky with no donkey dung visible.

He took a cab to see the Pyramids at Giza, and says, "put an Egyptian in the driver's seat and he shows all the calm and consideration of a hooded swordsman delivering Islamic justice . . . our driver raced through one red light after another." And once they arrived, "hustlers enveloped us the moment we climbed from the taxi offering rides on (camels) so decrepit that they could have been dragooned from the Egyptian Museum." Further, "con artistry at the Pyramids represents the most dynamic sector of the Egyptian economy." At the Pyramid of Cheops "the pleas for money know no bounds."

3

4

One important thing about personal experience, of course, is that it can be dangerous to generalize from it, and if you're an "influencer" like Horwitz became, what you say can have, well, a big influence on what people think. My influence is not such as to balance his, but I do feel obliged to say that my experience of Cairo, and Egypt generally, was very different. When my wife and I arrived at the Cairo airport we took a cab to our hotel near Giza, and our driver, who didn't remind me of a hooded swordsman, said he would meet us the following morning to take us to the Pyramids, which he did. When we arrived, there were no "aggressive hustlers," and the obligatory (short) camel ride was on a reasonably healthy looking animal (figure 3). The camel owner insisted he take a picture; I don't honestly remember him asking for money, but I'm sure he did.

5

Cairo did then have, and I'm sure does still have, parts that can be described as "exotic" and "colorful" especially in and around the Khan-el-Khalili bazaar. Figure 4 is a picture of a hookah shop, and figure 5 is another of the interesting places there. You might be able to just make out the little "we accept Visa" card just to the left of the doorway.

Horwitz mentions interviewing the famous Egyptian Nobel Prize winning author Naguib Mahfouz in the Ali Baba Cafe which was "perhaps least pleasant spot in the entire world." It was razed as part of a redevelopment project, but he did also spend time at Fishawy's Cafe in the Bazaar which he describes as "a back alley teahouse that had been open 24 hours a day for 200 years without evidence of a single renovation." My wife and I also spent some time there just because of its reputation for antiquity and figure 6 is a picture of what it looked like back then. It has, maybe because of his comments, been "renovated" as you can see in figure 7. The atmosphere there now is not much different than that at the 150 year old Sant Eustachio Cafe in Rome, or even the

100 year old Deux Magots in Paris - and it wasn't really *that* much different when Horwitz and I were there.

As a matter of fact, much of the rest of the book makes Cairo almost look like Paradise - the bloody hospitals of Yemen, the bloody battlefields and paranoia of Iraq, the idiocy of Khadafi, the leprosy of the Sudan, etc. a lot of which is funny in a tragi-comic sort of way. What's really amazing is that he went through all that when he didn't really have to! He could have just stayed in Cairo!

Doing Time in Provence
A Commentary on *A Year in Provence* by Peter Mayle

Why is it that a book called *A Year in Provence* seems much more interesting than one called *A Year in Kansas City*? Is it enough to say it's self-evident? A lot of our preferences are, of course, difficult to explain or justify in so many words, and, although it does seem like there might be something that could be said about this, I'm not sure it would sound at all convincing; this kind of thing is not a lot different than the old why do you prefer bourbon to scotch issue. In a few pages I'll be talking about Paul Hofmann's *The Seasons of Rome* and I suppose that title would attract readers who would know about the city and its long history and would therefore find it interesting to read about someone's experiences there, but I doubt most of the people who buy the book - or even those who visit the city really know very much about it, and even fewer will know anything about Provence.

A lot of book reading is certainly a form of escape, and a lot of it is just meant to satisfy our curiosity about something and/or add to our knowledge, and a book like Mayle's has the advantage of being both escape reading and curiosity satisfying reading. Obviously the quality of the writing matters too, and I've often claimed that a genius can make a masterpiece out of anything; I wouldn't call this book a masterpiece, or Peter Mayle a genius, but the book is at least reasonably entertaining, and it might well be that if he had written *A Year in Kansas City* it would have been a bestseller.

There is a danger a book like this will come across as something colored with a little too much elitist snobbery - "Look what an interesting life I'm having, while you all are stuck in Peoria!" but Mayle has enough problems that I think the effect of this is minimal. The nearest town was Ménerbes which you can see in figure 1; figure 2 is a view

from Ménerbes toward the Luberon mountains and his farm was out there somewhere. In fact, although this looks like a nice area to visit, probably the main lesson to learn from *A Year in Provence* is - don't buy a house there!

Of course, Mayle does like a lot of things about Provence; for example, he likes the fireplaces and the "primitive" smell which they produce. A lot of cities have banned them in new construction, but the fact that ones operated by gas or electricity are still allowed seems to indicate that there is some recognition of their ability to produce a desirable psychological effect, even without the aroma.

Mayle talks a lot, not surprisingly considering where he is, about food and its psychological benefits. Not being concerned much with what are called healthy eating habits myself, I like the story about his dinner which started with three kinds of pizza and went on to rabbit and boar pâté, a pork based terrine, sausages, duck covered with gravy, all topped off with a rabbit casserole and for dessert an almond cream gâteau. That's not exactly an example of the Mediterranean diet, but just for the record, the average lifespan in Provence is 80. This all reminds me of my grandmother who always put butter on steak and lived to just short of 100. Mayle says he was living among people "whose interest in food verges on obsession." He says the French are "as passionate about food as other nationalities are about sports or politics" and even his floor-cleaner acquaintance was up on the latest Michelin and Gault & Millau ratings and must have spent all of his money in restaurants. It's not surprising to find a quote on the cover from Julia Child praising this book!

It's not unusual to hear cooking described as an art, and the kind of Provençal meals which Mayle sometimes describes do, one could claim, *sort* of stand to McDonald's as Bach stands to Lawrence Welk or Rembrandt to Chuck Close.

Mayle says that in Provence he learned that time is a very elastic commodity, and, e.g., *un petit quart d'heure* means "sometime today." Ah yes, the efficient Brit expat confronted with the laid-back charm of Provençal life. But it's hard to generalize from what's happened to one influential writer who had this kind of encounter with, in fact, very few Provençals. This kind of experience and the gestures which he describes that go with talk about time, are interesting, in any case, from the point of view of language analysis, and illustrate how complex communication can be. *Pour mémoire*, although I've only been in Provence as a tourist I don't remember ever running into any misunderstandings about time.

Predictably, he claims that not just Provençals but the French as a whole are even more dangerous as drivers than the notorious Italians! I've done a lot of driving in Europe - Palermo, Naples, Paris, or Provence, it's all pretty much the same, and I've always enjoyed it at least partly because I feel I can do anything I want as long as I don't hit anybody. There are obviously a lot of traffic laws in France, Italy and, of course, the U.S., to which little attention is paid. On highway 5 in California very few drivers are under the speed limit unless traffic has slowed them down.

He also complains about the roads being jammed with trailers, at least at certain times, but one thing *I've* always noticed about European roads in general is the relative *absence* of trailers, and certainly there are few of the giant motor homes which one encounters on California highways and running their generators in the campgrounds.

Mayle claims that "the most modern French cafe is quite likely to have a chamber of horrors in the back," the "chamber of horrors" being the *toilette à la Turque* - "a shallow porcelain tray with a hole in the middle and footrests at each side." I can only vaguely remember encountering one of these many years ago, and I don't think it was even in France. But, again, it's hard to judge from one person's experience, whether Mayles, mine, or whoever's. Anyway, despite the alleged omnipresent *toilette a la Turque*, Mayle says he's liked almost every cafe he's been to in France, and I'd agree with that.

I'd accuse him of making up the *toilette* episode with the comically fastidious English tourists. As I've said elsewhere, this kind of book is classified as non-fiction, but did he actually get out his notebook and write down the dialogue as it happened?

One of the things which certainly influenced Mayle and his wife to make their move was the difference in weather. Provence *can* be pretty cold in the winter - 30's are not unusual in some parts, and in the summer some places hit 90 pretty often, but on the whole I guess it's true that it's better than the "impenetrable cloud" of the English winter and the "damp summer." If you're working at an indoor job all day, weather may not matter so much; but if you're not, weather can be very important, and that's why a lot of places along the California coast are expensive - weather is one of the most important things to spend money on, and Mayle would obviously agree.

In closing, when a friend asked him if he ever got bored, he said, "We found the everyday curiosities of French rural life amusing and interesting," which sounds a little condescending - it almost sounds like he might have said it tongue-in-cheek.

A Year in Provence won the award for Best Travel Book from the British Book Awards in 1989, but I wouldn't really call it a "travel book;" a travel book is the kind of thing Rick Steeves writes - or H. V. Morton on a more sophisticated level.

A Commentary on *Driving over Lemons* by Chris Stewart

Chris Stewart is another expat Brit who moved off to buy a farm and live what his publisher calls an "enviable life" - the good, natural, green life - in his case in Spain south of Granada. He's kind of a strange fellow - a one time rock musician, and still a professional sheepherder and aspiring politician. He had also been a travel writer covering Spain, so I think he should have known more about what he was getting into. He compares his Spanish farm life favorably to that of, say "an insurance clerk working in an office," or a "besuited businessman waiting for the daily ride to the treadmill," but if he were honest I think there may have been some days he might have preferred an office to being covered with "a film of sweat and a cloud of flies" or having the wind blow through his house so hard it knocked the furniture over,

or having to pour boiling water on the walls to get rid of the scorpions.

He could apparently walk from the town of Orgiva (fig. 1) to his new home, and Expira, one of his neighbors comments on the nice view even though, as she swats away a cloud of flies with a dishcloth, she says "life is nothing but drudgery and pain" and the middle of the day "like every other middle of the day, was scorching hot." And then there's the shower they have to walk a long way to use that has a dead goat hanging in it.

And, of course, his un-eco conscious fellow farmers blast their crops "with every fungicide and pesticide" they can lay their hands on.

When he needs help with work on the house, instead of putting an ad in the Granada newspaper *Ideal*, he gets in touch with his sister in London to hire two New Zealanders and send them! Stewart says he has worked with Kiwis in Britain, and admired their "propensity for hard work." No comment.

Twice a year he goes to Sweden to shear sheep for an entire month, but he doesn't like the "dreary landscape" with its "interminable pine forests," so I guess he was glad to get back to scorching heat, flies, bedbugs, and scorpions. On one occasion when he was off to Sweden his wife was pregnant and they were lucky to have neighbors who could help out in his absence, the New Zealanders, I guess, being of no use with this sort of thing. *Driving over Lemons* was his first book so he hadn't made anything from that source yet, and must have needed the sheep shearing money. Sheep shearing must be more difficult than it looks if you have to hire a guy all the way from southern Spain to do the job in Sweden!

In the last year before he finished the book there was pouring rain for weeks with 14 buckets and bowls around the house to catch the leaks. They had no telephone, their solar power attempt had failed, and the firewood was soaked. When summer finally came "the sweat pours off you while the frenzied screaming of the cicadas and other hot night creatures makes your head reel."

The Spanish farm food he encounters is not quite up to the standards Mayle found in food obsessed Provence - chicken heads, ham fat, pig blood pudding, prickly pear, stale bread, and brown (yes, brown) wine for what's called a "strong breakfast." That may explain why he apparently often got away to write a lot of the book in the more civilized Mirasierra Cafe (fig. 2) in Orgiva to which he refers as his "office".

2

To conclude, there is a clear difference between finding a book interesting to read and finding the life being lived by the characters in it to be one we would want to live ourselves. Zola writes interesting books, but no one wants to trade places with most of his important characters!

.   The book does end happily, as we could guess from the quotes on the cover, and that's nice; I can certainly see why it's subtitled "an optimist in Spain." A realist, let alone a pessimist, would have given up and moved to California - or at least Orgiva.

Figure 1 picture credit: José Antonio Berrocal Perez (CC BY-SA 4.0 DEED) https://commons.wikimedia.org/wiki/File:%C3%93rgiva,_en_Granada_%28 Espa%C3%B1a%29.jpg.

A COMMENTARY ON *SICILIAN ODYSSEY* BY FRANCINE PROSE

1

Francine Prose is a prolific writer who has won all sorts of awards but has written just one travel book, *Sicilian Odyssey*, covering a month she and her husband spent on the island where she says she wishes she'd been born. There are certainly a lot of reasons to visit it - beaches, food, and one of the most complex cultural histories you'll find in any part of Europe. Unlike the other so-called "travel books" discussions of which have preceded it in this volume, it is actually about *travel* - that is traveling around, in this case from Catania to Palermo and a lot of places more or less in between. The cover description says the book is illustrated with Prose's own photography, but don't look forward to the sometimes just bad or puzzling black and white pictures. I don't think she learned much from her photographer friend, Letizia Battaglia. This commentary is illustrated with, mostly, *my* pictures which are better.

2

Like most visitors to the island, they landed at Catania. She says it is "cursed with a reputation for petty crime, urban neglect, and pollution," so they go up the coast to Acireale where she reports on the *Carnevale*. Figure 1 is a picture of one of the typical float displays.

Although this kind of "local color" can be interesting to a degree, I think she should have said more about Catania, despite its alleged reputation which I don't

really think it has anymore. One of the interesting things about it is the way volcanic debris has been used over the centuries which gives a lot of the buildings a distinctive black and white look. Figure 2 is the Piazza del Duomo with the Cathedral on the left and figure 3 is a better picture of the Cathedral taken from the Ristorante del Duomo. The 13th century Castello Ursino seen in figure 4 which was built by the Emperor Frederick II is one of the few buildings in the city to have escaped major damage in the 1693 earthquake. It's now a museum with a lot of interesting things like the amazing *pietra dura* table in figure 5.

And speaking of amazing things, the Roman amphitheater *over* which part of the city was built has been undergoing on and off excavation for a long time; going down into the ruins is a memorable experience.

She complains right at the start that "driving anywhere in Sicily is not for the faint of heart," that the traffic in Palermo is "homicidal," and that the most vivid memories of her first trip to Sicily are of yanking her two young sons "out of the path of cars speeding in the wrong direction up one way streets."

As I've said before, it's dangerous to generalize from the experience of one person, whether hers or mine in this case, but I've also made two trips to Sicily and done a lot of driving all over it, including Palermo, and thoroughly enjoyed it.

She mentions seeing Etna from Taormina on her first trip, and figure 6 is a view of it - smoking away as it almost always is - from the Taormina Greek theater.

Figure 7 is a view of Ortigia, essentially an island attached to the mainland of Syracuse by a double causeway you can't see in this picture - but you can see Etna again in the distance. Prose calls Ortigia "one of the most appealing places in all of Sicily." She says she fantasizes about buying an abandoned palace there and fixing it up - sort of the thing Chris Stewart or Peter Mayle might try, except that Ortigia is very urban.

She mentions that Hiero II, the powerful ruler of Syracuse in the 3rd c. B.C. probably employed Archimedes to enlarge the suburban fortress of Castello Eurialo, but the gigantic Altar of Zeus near the city was also built in his day, and what remains of it can be seen in figure 8. It's usually called the largest "altar" ever built.

One of Prose's other non-fiction books is about Caravaggio and she spends about as much time talking about his *Burial of St Lucy* (fig. 9) as she does talking about anything else in Sicily. She says it's in the Galleria Regionale in Syracuse, but it has been moved back to the church in Syracuse for which it was painted, Santa Lucia al Sepolcro. "Nothing can prepare you," she says, "for the painting's force." For one thing, like a lot of his pictures, it's big - the figures are close to life-size. She calls it "the darkest and certainly among the most hopeless and least consoling of religious paintings," although "there is something comforting about its honesty." It doesn't seem like "comforting" is the right word. It's displayed behind the altar of the church now, so it's hard to get a good look at it, and the setting seems too light and white - and the way a painting is displayed *can* affect how we respond to it.

She mentions that Caravaggio is often given credit for naming "The Ear of Dionysus" (fig. 10), the amazing cave famous for its echoes which was apparently used as a prison by Dionysius I, but it's more famous as the place where the

Athenians captured after their failed attempt to take Syracuse in 413 were held, most of them dying there.

The Villa Romana del Casale, near Piazza Armerina, gets a few pages in the book and it really is one of the things anyone going to Sicily as a tourist should see. It contains the most extensive display of Roman mosaics anywhere in one building. To this day it isn't clear who owned the place, but it is certainly imperial in extent and decoration, despite being pretty much in the middle of nowhere. One mosaic she mentions is the strange 3-eyed Polyphemus being enticed to drink too much by Odysseus (fig. 11), and, of course, there are the ball playing "Bikini Girls" (fig. 12).

The most impressive part of the place to most people is the "Corridor of The Great Hunt" with animals being captured and presumably sent to Rome (fig 13, 14).

The man many, including Prose, give credit for the place is Maximian, whose career is too complicated to go into, but he was nominally Emperor of the Western Roman Empire as the partner of Diocletian in the East, for a time, and then had trouble with Constantine that ended in his forced suicide - so he didn't have much time to spend here, even if it was in some sense his.

It was Maximian's son Maxentius whom Constantine defeated in the famous Battle of the Milvian Bridge in 312. Prose says that after the death of Maximian, Constantine "took over the Villa Romana," which doesn't seem unlikely if it belonged to Maximian and perhaps his son, but I don't believe there is any evidence that Constantine was ever there.

The mosaics may have their critics as "works of art" but the overwhelming nature of the whole accomplishment - the amount of *work* if nothing else - makes it unforgettable.

Prose compares the African prostitutes she encounters to the animals in the mosaics being brought from Africa to entertain the Romans, but I don't think the women would want to be compared to entertaining

14

15

16

animals, even if Prose's intent is to convey sympathy.

The ruins of the town of Morgantina are just a few miles from the Villa Romana, and one of the things she brings up there is how it's been looted by antiquities dealers; it is, however, still a very interesting place to visit. You can see the site in figure 15 with Etna just barely visible as a pyramid shaped shadow behind the hill in the middle distance. In figure 16 you can see some of the hollow tubes used in the construction of the dome and barrel vault over the baths; they were among the earliest examples of these things. Looters apparently didn't think the tubes had much resale value.

She doesn't spend much time on the town of Cefalu which is another great place, but she does prefer the Cathedral (fig. 17) there to the Cathedral of Monreale (fig. 18) and the Palatine Chapel in Palermo (fig. 19) . I'll just mention that the Cathedral of Cefalu is in neither Janson nor Stokstad; Monreale is in the former, and the Palatine Chapel in the latter. Prose does, however, allow that they are also "magnificent," but she calls the mosaics in those churches "cinematic" and says that

the difference between them and the Cathedral of Cefalu is "almost like the difference between seeing some splashy Cecil B. DeMille epic when you're a child and contemplating an art masterpiece as an adult."

I must admit to being a fan of Cecil B. DeMille, and I do think overall Monreale is the most impressive place of the three, but I certainly agree that all three are magnificent.

Roger de Hauteville essentially took Sicily

from its Muslim rulers in the 11th century while his fellow Normans were conquering England. His son, Roger II, initiated the building of the Cathedral of Cefalu, and also commissioned the Palatine Chapel in Palermo. Roger II's grandson, William II, was the ruler of Sicily most responsible for theCathedral of Monreale. All three buildings are essentially late 12th century, give or take a few decades.

Prose thinks that the presence of so many mosaic subjects in Monreale and the Palatine Chapel creates a distraction from the central image of the Pantocrator

- a word derived from the Greek essentially meaning "all powerful." However, she says, there is nothing quite like Cefalu's Pantocrator. The face of Jesus is "commanding," "fascinating," and "psychologically complex."

She calls the 5th century B.C. Doric Temple at Segesta (fig. 20) "probably the most majestically sited" such temple, although it was left unfinished because of fighting between Segesta and Selinunte.

If anything, I think the surviving ruins of several buildings at Selinunte make it at least as interesting as Segesta, but she apparently didn't visit it; figure 21 is a picture of Temple C there.

One of the places she really liked is Erice on a mountain top near the west coast, and I agree it's a great place to visit. She says it's not for the acrophobic, but that's one of its charms. Fig 22 is a view from it toward Monte Cofano.

21

22

23

Her visit was in early Spring and it was chilly and foggy, but she also liked that and was glad she hadn't come in the summer when "the narrow streets and tiny piazzas are choked with traffic," and she makes fun of an American businessman who mispronounces the name of the town he's going to "buzz up" to see. I think she invented this episode; have you ever heard an American say "buzz up?" Anyway, when I was there in the summer it was *not* choked with traffic - or businessmen – or other tourists.

She apparently didn't visit Agrigento; it's not on her map at least, but its ruins are even more celebrated than those at either Segesta or Selinunte. Figure 23 is a picture of the so-called Temple of Concord there. The Agrigento Temple of Zeus would have been the largest Doric temple ever built, but it was never to be completely finished. The museum at the site has what's left of one of the giants which supported the roof (fig. 24); you can see a model of the temple at the right and these figures look tiny (fig. 25).

She also mentions the Ephebe of Agrigento in the museum and compares it very unfavorably to the 5th century B.C. Ephebe of Mozia (Motya) (fig 26) in the Whitaker Museum on the island of Mozia just off the

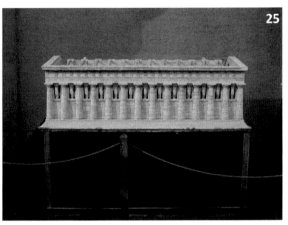

west coast. She says the latter stopped her short and she found it "so arresting and shockingly beautiful that it occurs to me that 2 hours from now the ferry could return and find us still standing here staring at the sculpture." Further, "there is nothing anywhere" like it "for not until Michelangelo would a sculptor again prove able to breathe so much life into marble." It *is* impressive, unusual, maybe almost unique, but it is not regarded as something quite so special by most authorities; it is not in either Janson or Stokstad, but it is in Richard Neer's standard text on *Greek Art and Archaeology*.

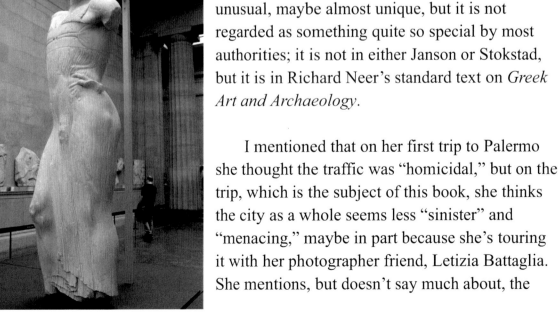

I mentioned that on her first trip to Palermo she thought the traffic was "homicidal," but on the trip, which is the subject of this book, she thinks the city as a whole seems less "sinister" and "menacing," maybe in part because she's touring it with her photographer friend, Letizia Battaglia. She mentions, but doesn't say much about, the

58

places that attract people interested in Palermo's past - The Cathedral, the Norman Palace, La Martorana, San Giovanni degli Eremiti, the Archaeological Museum, etc. but one thing she really loved is the Orto Botanico, and she quotes Goethe's claim that it is "the most beautiful place on earth.". Figure 27 is a picture of an ancient fig tree there. Most tourists don't spend much time in such places, but the one in Rome is also very impressive.

The one thing in Palermo on which she spends the *most* time is the ruined church of Santa Maria dello Spazio (fig. 28), the "Spazio" being the fainting spell Mary suffered at the Crucifixion. It's always difficult to put into words why some things or places affect us much more than they seem to affect others, why some things come to represent or inspire feelings in us that others just don't get. Anyway, she says it represents "the essence of what I'm looking for here, of what the Sicilians have, by necessity, learned how to do: to transmute the horrors of history into something extraordinary - and profoundly alive . . . it's the most beautiful place in Palermo."

Picture Credits: If no credit is given the picture was either taken by the author or is Public Domain Mark 1.

A Commentary on *The Seasons of Rome* by Paul Hofmann

'

The experiences which Paul Hofmann writes about are very different from those described by Stewart and Mayle. He was a well-off journalist, not a business suit rejecting farmer like them; he even lives on the same street as a former prime minister on the slopes of Monte Mario north of Vatican City. Figure 1 is a view from Monte Mario toward St. Peter's. On the cover of his book he is described as a

travel writer but, like Stewart and Mayle, he doesn't do much "traveling" - his book is all about his experiences in one city. It was published in 1997 when he was 85 and he lived to 97. the Mediterranean diet I guess.

At the beginning of the book he recounts an episode in which he and a bunch of other journalists are sitting around talking about where they would really like to live, and when he mentions that he lives in Rome they say "lucky you!" This struck me because once when there was a family gathering in Nashville where my aunt and uncle were well-traveled Vanderbilt professors, my aunt asked the same question and, after several votes for Paris, Hawaii, maybe even Rome, my grandmother's answer was - Carthage, Missouri! Although she had been living for several years with my aunt (her daughter) and uncle in Nashville, she had lived pretty much her whole life in Carthage, and for her places and things there carried an aura - memories, associations, etc. - that the Corso or Palatine Hill might for a Roman, or the Blvd. Saint-Germain or Montmartre for a Parisian. Not only places like Rome or Carthage can be somehow infused with this kind of value, all kinds of objects from works of art to old clothes can be - that's why your basement is probably full of what I'd just call stuff - the equivalent to Carthage in the world of stuff - but which for you is more like museum collection.

In attempting to explain why he likes Rome he says he likes the sunshine, cheap wine, tender artichokes, and the way Romans have of "arranging" things - of getting by, but that's just to say that it's hard to say why he *really* likes Rome - he could get all these things in Carthage. At this writing (11-28-23) the temperature in Carthage is the same as that in Rome - 60° with sunshine. I'm sure Two Buck Chuck is available and probably reasonably tender artichokes - he only mentions them once, so they can't have been *that* important to him. Actually he complains quite a bit about the climate - 100° heat and "weeks of uninterrupted hot weather," and then he's astonished that "sunny Italy could be so cold."

As far as "arranging" things goes, there probably isn't as much in Carthage that needs arranging. I bet that at least the mail service in Carthage is reliable, and problems with that are one of Hofmann's main complaints about life in Rome. It's interesting that out in rural Spain Chris Stewart in *Driving Over Lemons* has nothing but praise for the postal service and his mail person.

Like Mayle, he complains about the lack of precision in time talk - "punctuality," he says, "is not a Roman virtue." It's almost like there's some

genetic thing involved, but as I've mentioned elsewhere, although I haven't "lived" in the places they do, as a relatively long-term tourist I've never had any serious problem with temporal communication in either Provence or Rome.

He says he has access to "100 excellent

trattorias," and bountiful markets, so he's not in the position of Stewart being offered chicken heads for breakfast, but the Romans, based on what he says, are not "obsessed" with food like the French. One Roman treat which he mentions, and for which he seems to feel some contempt, is something my family always has around Christmas - *panettone*. He says many Romans eat it for breakfast and dessert from Christmas through March! He is a bit of a foodie which might partly explain his dislike of plebeian food like *panettone*. Two restaurants which he likes are near the Pantheon - *Fortunato's* and *Armando's* - each around $150 for a couple with full dinner and wine, which is about the going rate for well known Roman *ristoranti* - and the food *is* good. In figure 2 you're looking into the piazza from the porch of the Pantheon; Fortunato's is up the street on the far right and Armando's is offscreen down a street to the left.

He says that the dominant passions of the Romans are "automobiles, soccer, and television," and among those, based on what he goes on to say, soccer would be the thing with which Romans are *really* obsessed. Many Americans are certainly big sports fans, but in some European countries it seems soccer, or *calcio* or *fußball* or football is just about the most important thing in the lives of a lot of

people. The experience of going to, or watching on TV, a sports event of consequence to you, is a *little* like watching theater. I'm reminded of the reactions that sometimes occurred during 19th century performances as represented in Daumier's print (fig. 3) with people so caught up they're jumping out of their seats! I'm also reminded of the *émeute* that nearly overthrew the Emperor Justinian in Constantinople when he attempted to ban chariot racing because of the chaos created by supporters of the two primary teams.

I don't want to get too biological about this either, but it just seems that some people have the fan gene and some don't. My father who won a trophy as the best athlete in the city (St. Joseph, Mo.) couldn't have cared less about watching any sports event on TV, but his mother never missed a St. Louis Cardinals game on the radio and his wife (my mother) after moving to L.A. never missed a Lakers game on TV, even though neither one ever swung a bat or shot a basketball.

It irritates me that he accuses the 19th century German author Ferdinand Gregorovius of "turgid declamation" presumably referring to his most well known work, *History of Rome in the Middle Ages*, but his large *Wanderjahre in Italien* - it's hard to find in translation - is very interesting, and is actually what should be called a "travel book" but I think that term has become irrevocably attached to the kind of thing Hofmann - and Mayle and Stewart, *inter alios* - have written.

4

It's also odd that he pairs Giotto with Luca Signorelli when the latter is ordinarily considered far less important and is not even mentioned in Stokstad's gigantic *Art History.* He's also not even given an index entry in Hofmann's own book! He also refers to Rimini (fig. 4) as an "Adriatic backwater" What do you think? It's one of the biggest resorts in the whole country!

One of the most bizarre things on which he comments is the arrival of hundreds of thousands of starlings every fall (fig. 5), and the Romans have yet to find a way to prevent this. It has apparently been going on to a greater or lesser degree since antiquity when Pliny the Elder refers to them. How do they all find

enough to eat? And in winter? And if they come because it's warmer, why don't they go farther south?

And, of course there are also the stray cats, 200,000 or so according to Hofmann, for which Rome is famous. They're mostly taken care of by *gattare* or "cat lovers" around the city and the city hall bureaucrat in charge of animal rights.

I don't understand economics at all. Hofmann says that close to half of all Romans live on a government pension of some sort, many retiring in their forties or even thirties! I mentioned that Mayle said France leads the world in bureaucracy, but Hofmann calls Rome "the citadel of bureaucracy." In a discussion

somewhat related to this kind of thing, he talks about strikes and labor unions and mentions the Piazza Esedra as a frequent focal point of demonstrations and as a not very attractive place near the railroad station, but in my limited experience I don't recall anything unattractive about it. It's a popular

tourist area with the church of Santa Maria degli Angeli for which Michelangelo is given some credit at the left in figure 6 and the National Museum in the Baths of Diocletian behind with the sun on it. The railroad station is offscreen to the right.

As I mentioned, he appreciates good restaurants, and he also mentions two of the city's most famous coffee and tea spots - the Caffè Greco and Babington's. The former is on the Via Condotti near the Spanish Steps - it's where the white awning is on the right beyond Prada and across from Bulgari which is next to Gucci!(fig. 7). In its 250 year history The

Caffè Greco has been patronized by a long list of people in the arts, including Goethe, Stendahl, Keats, Byron, Bizet, Brahms, Joyce, Mark Twain,

Ingres, and Orson Welles.

In figure 8 Babington's is just to the left of the Spanish Steps with the house where Keats died at 25, now the Keats-Shelley Museum, on the right. Babington's, founded in 1893, has attracted a lot of movie stars including Richard Burton and Elizabeth Taylor.

About equally venerable is Giolitti's which is famous for its gelato; its near the Palazzo Montecitorio, the home of the Chamber of Deputies, and, according to Hofmann, is often full of the said deputies

One thing that most Americans ignore is the fact that the Magi brought their gifts to the Baby Jesus 12 days after Christmas on January 6, Epiphany, a word derived from the Greek φαίνειν,"to appear." In primarily Catholic places Epiphany is an important day of celebration, and in Rome a witch called a *Befana* (a corruption of "Epiphany") riding a broomstick is said to bring gifts to children on the eve of Epiphany. We, of course, on the other hand, associate a witch riding a broomstick with the eve of All Saints Day or Hallow's Eve, i.e., Halloween. And how did the witch get involved with Epiphany? "Good question," says Hofmann. And how did Santa Claus get involved with Christmas? That would take a doctoral thesis to sort out. Anyway, there is a big festival associated with the *Befana* in Piazza Navona (fig. 9) every January 6

10 As one would expect, he complains, like many others, about the "marble monstrosity" known as the Vittorio Emanuele Monument which is pretty much the most dominant thing in the city with the possible exception of the Colosseum. Maybe someday it will be more accepted - like the Eiffel Tower which was once considered appalling by many Parisians. Hofmann, in fact, makes fun of all the other monuments and commemorative plaques all over Rome honoring people about whom no one remembers anything.

He talks briefly about 4 hotels he singles out as "luxury" : the Grand, now called the St. Regis, the Hassler, the Excelsior, and the Lord Byron. He mentions some famous people who have stayed in them, but the first two are over $1000/night and the last two 3 or 4 hundred, so, unless you're at least *pretty* famous, look elsewhere. There are a lot of very fine hotels in Rome within my price limit of *around* $200/night.

He complains about motor scooters in general and Vespas in particular because they are used by bag-grabbers and are noisy and dangerous to pedestrians, but they are certainly a relatively efficient way to get around car-jammed cities, and are sometimes ridden by responsible people (see back cover).

He doesn't talk much about art but he does call the *Capitoline She-Wolf* (fig. 11) his favorite work of sculpture. He claims to have spent hours staring at it, and says "it stirs me more deeply . . .than . . . Michelangelo's *Pieta*." I would suppose he says this because he associates it with Roman antiquity, but he doesn't emphasize that, and essentially just describes it. *Chacun à son goût*, again, I guess. Anyway, more about art shortly.

A Commentary on *Paris* By John Russell

John Russell, who died in 2008, was a long time art critic for the NY Times and wrote several books, mostly on modern art. I don't know how much time he actually spent in Paris, but he says his first visit was 50 years before the book was published, or at least before it was written. He says he was wearing the peaked cap, blazer, and knee length gray flannel trousers which were the mark of his school in London, and this kept him from passing as a Parisian, but then he goes on to talk as though he were an adult at the time and went to a "famous cafe in Montmartre and called for pen, ink, and paper" and they were brought to him. So how old really was he? In his twenties and wearing a peaked cap and knee length trousers? His wife, Rosamond Bernier, who wrote the Foreword to the book, says it was first published in 1960 - 50 years before that Russell hadn't even been born yet! She also says they made a trip "to gather the illustrations." I don't know what "gather" means here; I'm not sure that they actually took *any* of the pictures in the book.

They are both name droppers in, however, two different senses. She brags about her encounters with Sartre and Simone de Beauvoir, Alice B. Toklas, Nancy Mitford, Picasso, Matisse, Giacometti, *inter alia*. Then, finally, in the last couple of paragraphs, she says her husband wrote a good book, and that to read it is like "sauntering through the city." I think if you read it, you'll think "saunter" isn't the right word. It's very detailed and intense.

As I said, Russell himself is a name dropper, but the names he drops are of people I've never heard of - Courteline? Littre? Pailleron? The "great historian" Louis Hautecoeur, by whom there is apparently not even anything in print? The book lacks footnotes and a bibliography so if you read it you'll just have to trust he's using legitimate sources. Some pages aren't even numbered for no apparent reason. This all means that the book isn't a work of scholarship in the narrow sense, but, as I said, it is dense and full of information. It's certainly not a book you'd want to carry around the way you'd carry around the ordinary tourist guide, nor is it a "travel book" like the ones discussed earlier, although it has a little more in common with Francine Prose's book than it does with the others. It really presupposes you already have some sense of what Paris is like at least physically, and likewise it presupposes a somewhat more than rudimentary knowledge of the history of French civilization. It also presupposes you have a dictionary and can look up words like ebullition, insolite, vespertinal, enskied, and Daedalian. Actually, I suppose if you're inclined to read books like this you probably already *do* know what these words mean.

He says that at least before he made that first trip at whatever age wearing whatever clothes, he had "read all that there was to read," about Paris, so, again, he must have been at least an adult. However, a couple of pages later he says that according to the catalog of the British Library, "the Parisian guidebook has a history almost as long as that of Paris itself," and I doubt he read *all* of that before he made his first trip.

Like a lot of authors of books about places they've visited, he likes to generalize, or lead us to generalize, regarding national, or in this case civic, character traits. He says "insofar as there is a specifically Parisian turn of mind, it's fundamentally dismissive. You will never hear from a Parisian cab driver the equivalent of the cry "Ecco Roma!" as he points to some "hallowed sight." How many taxis have you taken in Rome? Ever hear one say that? He says "Parisians are inquisitive by nature . . . they are not passive." There are 11 million people in Paris - how many have you studied? interviewed? watched? And then 4 pages or so later he says, Parisians "defy generalization."

There is something to his claim that there is a difference between Paris and places like Venice and Florence which he says are "mummified" *villes d'art*, but "mummified" is obviously too pejorative. Part of the difference is simply due to the fact that Paris is a much bigger city and the sights that attract the tourists are farther apart - and there is also a lot more non-tourist business going on.

He says that it is the "refusal to give in to the past that dissuades so many visitors from the orthodox routine of the sightseer." But then he says it's only in places like the Louvre, Notre Dame, Les Invalides, etc. that we find "the seeker for knowledge" - but these *are* the things on the "orthodox routine." This whole paragraph on page 19 doesn't make sense to me.

He can be very unfriendly to some Parisian monuments: "Sacre Coeur is ridiculous," and "the steeples of Sainte-Clotilde (fig. 1) look like German jewelry," and "the towers of Saint-Sulpice look like municipal inkwells," and "the Sorbonne is ugly beyond belief." However, he says he likes visiting the churches, at least "after a long absence," anyway. He doesn't really explain this, but I think it simply has to do with what these places, regardless of what they look like, "represent" either in his life or the life of the history of Paris - and an awful lot of what is valued in the history of art, architecture, and things in our lives in general, is not easy to describe as "beautiful."

He talks later a little about the Bastille and what it represented, and how its cannons "became a symbol of the enemy" and it was because the Bastille itself was a symbol that it was attacked; the number of actual prisoners on July 14, 1789 was apparently between 4 and 7, and Louis XVI had already scheduled it for demolition. The Communards pulled down the Vendome Column a century later for the same reason - it was a *symbol*, it *represented* the enemy.

He devotes a short chapter to the Comédie-Française, and he claims "there are more great plays in the French language than in any other," and he can quote Lord Chesterfield to support him, but they may be the only 2 English speakers, at least, who think this. Moliere is the only French author of comedies I might put on the same shelf with Sheridan, Congreve, Goldsmith, etc., but Shakespeare is altogether on a different level from Racine and Corneille. Anyone who can sit through 2 or 3 hours of rhymed couplets deserves an award - and, of course, it's virtually impossible to translate rhymed couplets so that they're rhymed couplets in English which means that unless you understand 17th century spoken French, forget it -

you're not even in a position to judge a performance. It should be said that it is always difficult to judge the literature of a language you don't understand well, whether spoken or written, but I'd be willing to bet that, for example, there are at least ten public performances of plays by Shakespeare in Germany for every one by Racine.

The Paris Opera Garnier (fig. 2) is a much more spectacular place than the theater of the Comédie-Française. Russell calls it " the grandest, most ample, and most conspicuous thing of its kind," but its position in the world of French culture has fallen to the point that, he says, "it's hardly more relevant than the former stock exchange in Moscow." He apparently wrote the book before the Opera Bastille (fig. 3) was finished, and it has certainly had its share of problems both administrative and structural, and, although it was meant to be

exclusively for opera with the Palais Garnier to be only for ballet, etc., operas are now being staged in the latter once again. Opera offers a dramatic form of escape and the Opera Garnier contributes much more to this than the conservatively modern and sterile Opera Bastille.

He also claims that "Parisians have movie fever the way the Spaniards have bull fever." This is an odd comparison, but, in any case, bullfights have now been banned in some major Spanish cities. Anyway, movies are, of course, a kind of escape vehicle like all forms of theatrical entertainment - and like the arts in general.

4 He talks in a couple of places about cafes - those that were popular in the 19th century with people like Manet, e.g., Tortoni's which is gone, and the Deux Magots that's still there on the Place Saint-Germain-des-Prés and which was, says Russell, "for the people of my generation the true center of Paris." In figure 4 the Deux Magots is on the right with the green awnings, and the Cafe de Flore, which he also mentions, is at the far left. The Flore says Sartre and Simon de Beauvoir preferred it. The Deux Magots claims Guillaume Apollinaire, Andre Gide, and Hemingway, although the latter was more often to be found at the Closerie des Lilas which also still exists in Montparnasse. In *A Movable Feast* he says that the Closerie was where he spent most of his time. One could rent a cheap room and then spend all day in a cafe. Russell quotes Sartre who says the same thing about Le Dôme which also still

exists; he says he "lived" there in the thirties. All these places are much more expensive now, especially if you're eating dinner in them, but an espresso at the Deux Magots isn't much more than it is at Peet's. Their menus are all online of course.

One of the longest chapters is devoted to the Louvre (fig. 5) to which he refers as a "municipal carcass" that has been "robbed of its humanity," because "the visitor's homage is paid not to the building but to the works of art it happens to house," about which he says nothing. Moreover, the visitors make up "a listless throng" afflicted with what he calls "museum foot." Well, what else would you want it to be? Public housing? A bureaucratic complex where people would suffer from "office foot"? I think the art museum function is, in fact, perfect for the Louvre, and *keeps it* from being a "carcass," and I think it's likely that more people know something about *its* history than they do about, for example, the history of the Uffizi in Florence, the Zwinger in Dresden, or the Vatican Museum building. Most famous museums were not built to *be* museums, at least not public ones.

One place in Paris which *was* actually built to be a museum is the Centre National d'Art et de Culture Contemporain Georges Pompidou or Beaubourg as it is usually called (fig. 6) which Russell says "is like nothing else in Paris." If the Louvre is a carcass, the Beaubourg is a skeleton. Like the Eiffel Tower, it has provoked a lot of controversy, not least over the amount of money spent on it - probably around a billion dollars after the repairs that are apparently going to require it to be closed for several years soon. That would buy the whole collection of some museums. So unfortunately you may not be able to see the Circle Composition of Genevieve Assize (fig. 7) or Joan Miró's Blue II (fig 8) for some time.

7

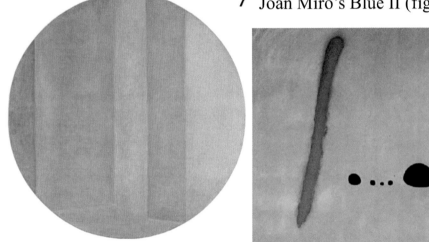

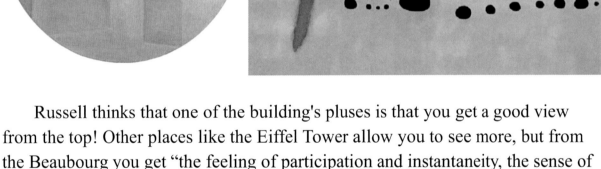

8

Russell thinks that one of the building's pluses is that you get a good view from the top! Other places like the Eiffel Tower allow you to see more, but from the Beaubourg you get "the feeling of participation and instantaneity, the sense of being aloft and yet within hallooing distance of the ground," whatever that means.

He thinks that one of the things that turns Parisians off about the Beaubourg is that it exposes what is supposed to be covered up - plumbing, air vents, heating equipment, etc. In another generalization he claims that Parisians are "secretive," and this display of what should be hidden is therefore abhorrent to them. As he says nothing about the contents of the Louvre, he says nothing about what's in the Beaubourg either, which I do think is more justifiable.

He describes the Carnavalet Museum as "one of the most delightful and amusing of all museums," and as "par excellence the Parisian's own museum," but,

9

again, he hardly touches on what's there. I think of it as a kind of elegant attic where evocative mementoes of one kind or another, rather than important works of art, are kept. Among the most interesting things are the reconstructed rooms taken from mostly now demolished townhouses, though some of the buildings themselves are still standing.

10

In one place he describes the Palais Royal as "deserted" and in another as just having shops with "old stamps, colonial campaign medals, and art nouveau exercise books." I'm not sure when he wrote this, but it's now full of fashionable boutiques - Marc Jacobs is now where Camille Desmoulins made his famous call to arms speech at the start of the Revolution. I've been there quite a few times since 1975 and never thought of it as deserted.

The square in the oldest section (fig.9) is now occupied by a bunch of squat columns which people mistake for an art installation; the columns were actually just meant to keep people from parking there.

He says that there are several things wrong with the Place des Vosges (fig. 10), but he really only talks about one - "the savorless *jardin publique*" where you can't even play croquet anymore! That's even worse than not being able to park in the Palais Royale. He does admit that the original plan of Henry IV c. 1600 has survived, and that's why most people visit this part of Paris. One of the pieces which survives was the home of Victor Hugo and it's now a museum devoted to him.

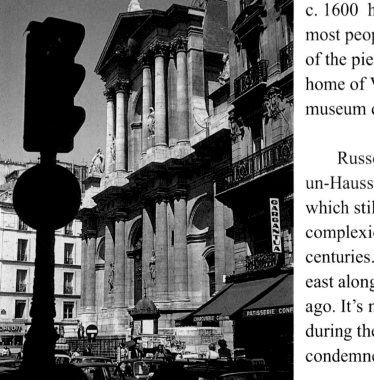

Russell devotes a chapter to the un-Haussmannized Rue Saint-Honoré which still owes "its present complexion" to the 17th and 18th centuries. In figure 11 you're looking east along it as it appeared a few years ago. It's now one-way going east but during the reign of terror for the condemned it was one-way going west -

down this street and around the corner to what's now called the Place de la Concorde where the guillotine was.

One of the interesting places on the street is the church of Saint-Roche (fig. 12) where a lot of important people are buried including Corneille, Diderot, and a fellow named Duguay-Trouvin whom Russell describes as "the greatest of seabears," and that term is in no dictionary I can find. Since he was a great slave trader and pirate it seems appropriate though.

He says that it was from its facade that Napoleon repulsed a royalist attack in October 1795, but according to the engraving by Charles Monnet which is always used to illustrate this event, the royalists were occupying the church and Napoleon's men were firing *at* it. In any case, the fighting was spread all around the area and not confined to the front of the church.

Russell says that Poussin "was delighted to be called back from Rome" after establishing himself there as a popular painter, but the usual view is that he *didn't* want to go back to Paris. Guizot, in his *History of France* says that he returned like one "sentenced to be sawn in half!" Russell, like Kenneth Clark (see p. 16)

compares Seurat (about whom he wrote a whole book) to Poussin which, if not a mistake, is, again, a really unusual pairing.

A clearer mistake may be his claim that the fellow reading in the center of the picture of the salon of Mme. Geoffrin by Lemonnier (fig. 13) is d'Alembert, but the usual view is that the reader is an actor named LeKain, and d'Alembert is to the right of this fellow at the corner of the table.

A picture is described as a view from "from Notre-Dame toward Saint-Julien-le-Pauvre," but it isn't. Saint-Julien is across the river from Notre-Dame and there aren't any buildings between Notre-Dame and the river, and in the picture all we see are rooftops (page 250).

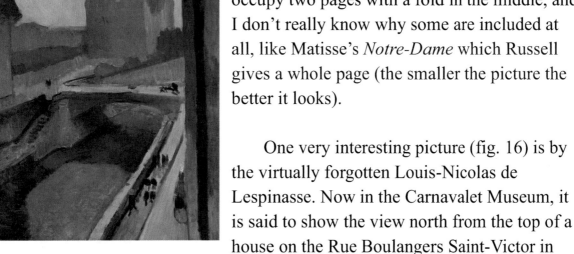

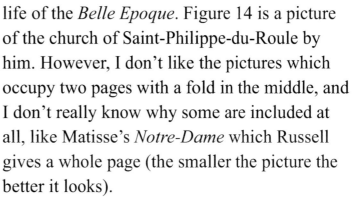

One good thing about the book, however, is that it does in fact have a lot of very good pictures, including four of paintings by Jean Beraud who is certainly one of the painters who best documents the social life of the *Belle Epoque*. Figure 14 is a picture of the church of Saint-Philippe-du-Roule by him. However, I don't like the pictures which occupy two pages with a fold in the middle, and I don't really know why some are included at all, like Matisse's *Notre-Dame* which Russell gives a whole page (the smaller the picture the better it looks).

One very interesting picture (fig. 16) is by the virtually forgotten Louis-Nicolas de Lespinasse. Now in the Carnavalet Museum, it is said to show the view north from the top of a house on the Rue Boulangers Saint-Victor in

1786, but I don't recognize anything. Nevertheless, it is really hard to believe it isn't a photograph. The original in the Carnavalet Museum is about 4 feet wide and is described as a colored gouache (more or less opaque watercolor). Amazingly, he made many such pictures.

16

And just for the record Georges Braque (e.g., fig 17) got a state funeral in front of the Louvre presided over by Andre Malraux himself. It may sound odd to say so, but work like Braque's and Matisses's is very conservative - it's what's favored by the established critics, like Malraux and Russell; it's the kind of thing collectors will therefore pay millions of dollars for. No one even knows where an anti-establishment radical like Lespinasse is buried.

"Paris as we know it," says Russell, " is very largely the creation of (Baron Georges) Haussmann," whom he calls "one of the most obnoxious of recorded beings." He buys into the theory that one of the main motives for Haussmann's work was the hope of reducing the number of "inaccessible barracks and Daedalian roadways" which were useful to revolutionaries during insurrections. I think this might well have been a consideration, but Haussmann was also involved with things like water supply, sewage removal, making gas available for stoves and lights, improving transportation generally, using street number addresses, etc.

Russell accuses him of "butchery" and he thinks that the Rue Saint-Antoine is "the most beautiful street in Paris partly at least because "Haussmann never got

Blvd. Haussmann

anywhere near it." However he does admit that even Victor Hugo acclaimed "the Paris of Haussmann," and he says that the broad, straight, tree-lined avenues, e.g., as in figure 18 "have turned out to adapt themselves rather well to changes in fashion," and "with every year that passes Haussmann on balance looks more and more like a true friend of Paris." As it's fair to say Russell was.

CREDITS

A Commentary on *A Stranger in Spain* by H.V. Morton

H.V. Morton dropped out of school at 16, and at 18 went to work for the newspaper in Birmingham England of which his father was the editor. In 1923 he covered the opening of the tomb of King Tut for the London Daily Express which did a lot to establish his reputation, and soon after that he began writing the books for which he is still well-known - what are called "travel books" like *A Stranger in Spain*, which is the record of one of his later adventures; it was published in 1955. He wrote an amazing number of such books, and for someone who didn't even finish high school he had an amazing knowledge of European, and especially British, history. He does say, however, that "the Spanish schoolboy has a more involved history to learn than any other European," and I think that's a fair claim, but I also think Morton likely knew more about the history of their country than most Spaniards, whether schoolboys or adults.

He began his visit, like most tourists, in Madrid, where few things which the tourist wants to see have changed much since he was there. What *has* changed is the attention given to some social conventions like the evening *paseo*, the circulation of a large part of the population to take the evening air, or something like that, which has pretty much faded away now, as has the near impossibility of being served in a restaurant before 10 PM which he encountered. I've also never seen the whispering pen vendors which he complains "haunted the streets."

He visited the Royal Armory where he saw what he says is the armor worn by Charles V in the famous picture by

Titian (fig 1) which shows the emperor at the Battle of Muhlberg. However, the armor on display which is called the Muhlberg Armor (fig. 2) doesn't really look like the armor Charles is wearing in the picture - although it is hard to tell from these photos - and the Prado where the picture is, doesn't claim that it's the same. In any case, Morton calls the painting "one of the greatest pictures ever painted."

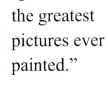

He does spend a little time on a few of the other pictures in the Prado, but he's more interested in history than art. He makes the standard claim that Goya's portrait in the Prado of *Charles IV and His Family* (fig. 3) makes them all look like dunces or worse, but the truth is that usually when we know someone is a jerk we tend to think a portrait makes the subject *look* like a jerk. I've talked more about this elsewhere, but if I could tell you that King Charles (fig. 4) led the troops to victory at the Battle of Tijuana, that he gave over the Palace of San Ildefonso to the homeless, etc., you'd probably think he looked better than "blunt" and "stupid." Likewise we know that his wife Maria Luisa (fig. 4 also) was not the finest of

women, but does she really look like "one of Cinderella's ugly sisters, a greedy termagant?"(fig. 4) I don't know if the king's daughter and her husband at the far right (fig. 5) are "not idealized or flattered," as Morton claims, but they do look royal enough, and even the king's worthless son, the future Ferdinand VII, looks fine (fig. 6, in blue). The only subject in the picture who really *does* look suspicious is Goya himself in the back at his easel.

Morton says that the portrait of Mary Tudor by the Dutch born Antonio Moro, as he was known in Spain, is "wonderful," and "famous," but I don't know how famous it really is. I do, however, think Moro, who did portraits of important people all over Europe, is an underrated painter.

Another Prado painting he discusses is *Las Meninas* by Velazquez (8), and he says that the self-portrait included (fig. 9) is "one of the greatest things in the Prado."

He also refers to the portrait of Philip IV's son Carlos by Velazquez (not shown) as a picture of "perhaps the best known royal child in art," but I think that honor should go to his sister Margarita Teresa (fig. 10) in *Las Meninas*.

The works of art on which he probably spends the most time of all are the 15th c. tapestries in the Parochial Museum in Pastrana, east of Madrid. They depict the expedition of Alfonso V of Portugal to North Africa and the occupation of Tangier among other successes. As I said, he knows a lot about English history and one thing he brings up in Pastrana is that Alfonso V is the

grandson of Philippa of Lancaster, the daughter of John of Gaunt, and one of her sons was Henry the Navigator, so even he was partly English! These tapestries were made in Tournai from designs by the Portuguese court painter, Nuño Gonzálvez, but how they got to Pastrana isn't clear.

He went then to visit the Escorial (fig. 12) and says that it's more like Philip II than Versailles is like Louis XIV. I do think that both places reflect quite a bit of the personality of their most famous residents; the splendid lifestyle of Louis XIV is well enough known, and Philip's *was* very different. The Escorial, at least the part before the Bourbons arrived, is very plain compared to Versailles, and it's said that Philip himself usually looked so plain that people would sometimes walk right by him without realizing who he was.

Even the throne room (fig. 13) would hardly be judged worthy of the Count of Pamplona, let alone appropriate for the at least nominal ruler of more of the world than anyone else. I'm calling this the throne room, but over the past few decades what counts as the throne room seems to have varied, and when this picture was taken the throne wasn't in this room, although it has been there in the past. In any case, its appearance is consistent with the relatively modest atmosphere authorities associate with Philip's part of the Escorial.

One interesting thing he saw in the Basilica of the Escorial was the tomb of José Antonio Primo de Rivera, one of the heroes of the Franco *Falange Espagnola*. After Morton wrote this book, his body was moved to the nearby less prestigious Valley of the Fallen, which is a controversial place for a lot of reasons. In 2019 Franco's own body was taken from the latter monument because it was argued that it was becoming too much a place of veneration devoted to a dictator. He was reburied in a family cemetery. José Antonio was removed from The Valley of the Fallen also and reburied in the modest San Ildefonso cemetery in Madrid just this year (2013).

The one painting in the Escorial he talks about is El Greco's *Martyrdom of St. Maurice* (fig. 14), and he quotes Julius Meier-Graefes *Spanische Reise* in translation - it is "the most beautiful picture of mankind" which is a bad translation of the German; the painting's *subject* is not "mankind," what he *means* is simply that it's the most beautiful picture anyone has ever painted. *Über Geschmack lässt sich nicht streiten.*

He also praises the Escorial library which *is* a fine place. He draws particular attention to the collection of the manuscripts of St. Teresa's work; Philip was an admirer, and got her and her order out of a jam or two.

One point I've made elsewhere is that what makes an original work of art so much more valuable that a copy from which it is visually indistinguishable is the context which the original represents, and which to some extent is evoked by it. In

a *somewhat* similar way, when you know the history of a place, its historical context - say a piece of landscape where a battle was fought, or a building where important things happened or where important people lived - these become much more interesting than if you were just studying them because of an interest in geography or architecture. The Escorial, of course, is a place with which many visitors can associate a lot of Spanish history; a less obviously historically evocative place back in Madrid is the "House of the 7 Chimneys"(fig. 15) which was the residence of the English Ambassador John Digby, Earl of Bristol, in 1623 when the future Charles I and the Duke of Buckingham arrived to try to arrange the former's marriage to the daughter of Philip IV. This ended in awkward failure, but the story provoked Morton's encounter with the building which makes it much more interesting than just another example of period architecture would be.

In Toledo he devoted most of his time to the Cathedral. He mentions that the spectacular *retablo* behind the altar (fig. 16) must have served like sort of an illustrated

newspaper for people who couldn't read. This is the kind of thing often said about elaborate stained glass windows - "they were the Bible of the poor" - but the truth is that even graduate students in theology today often have trouble deciphering the subjects. One interesting image among the figures to the right, he's on the left in figure 17, is said to represent Saint Abu Walid who, although a Muslim, is given credit for saving the life of the Christian Bishop of the city; Morton tells the story of how this happened.

He spends quite a bit of time on the Capilla de Los Reyes Nuevos, again because of the English connection. In figure 18 you see the sarcophagi of Henry II of Castile and his wife Joan. Catherine of Lancaster (fig. 19) and her husband Henry III, the son of Henry II, are entombed on the other side of the chapel. Catherine of Lancaster was the daughter of John of Gaunt, and so the granddaughter of Edward III. Catherine's son was Juan II, the father of Isabella who married Ferdinand. Morton doesn't stop there, but I will.

He passes very quickly over Goya's *Betrayal of Christ* and El Greco's *Disrobing of Christ* in the Sacristy/Treasury. The Goya picture isn't considered one of his more important, but the *Disrobing* is very important as El Greco's first big

success in Spain and one of the most important of all of his pictures (fig. 20). The commission was a product of his friendship with Luis de Castilla whom he had met in Rome and who was the son of the Dean of the Cathedral. Sometimes, as here, Morton does betray a lack of perspective when it comes to the visual arts; if El Greco had been the nephew of the daughter of a sister of the King of England, he would have been given more attention.

He attended a celebration of the Mozarabic Liturgy in the Mozarabic Chapel of the Cathedral, the only place where this celebration occurs on a daily basis. The chapel is under the south tower of the Cathedral, on the right in figure 21. The Mozarabic Liturgy is, like the Ambrosian variant which survives in Milan, a non-Gregorian Liturgy approved by the Vatican.

Morton says that during the Spanish Civil War the Cathedral's treasures were hidden in tunnels under what is now called El Greco's

21

22

House. He doesn't say any more about the building, but it is now an interesting museum. El Greco did live more or less where the museum is for 27 years, but this building was a ruin before it was "restored" in the 20th c.

As I said, he barely mentions El Greco's *Disrobing* in the Cathedral, and likewise simply says that he saw his *Burial of The Conde de Orgaz* (fig. 22) in El Greco's parish church, Santo Tomé. Again, it's his prerogative to put history over art, but a painting as important as this one - as important as any in Spain - counts as something an historian could justify saying a little more about.

He visited the Roman theater in Merida (fig. 23), and calls it "one of the most complete I have ever seen," but if he had seen it before its "restoration" (fig. 24) he might have thought differently. It's often a little disappointing to learn just how extensively some ancient buildings have been restored.

Moving on to Seville, he comments on the prevalence of buses full of tour groups and claims that "the individual traveler is a complete anomaly." I don't know what it was like in the 1950's, but individual travelers are certainly not

"anomalies" in places like Seville today, although tour buses are also certainly still to be seen.

As most writers who cover Seville do, Morton emphasizes the size of the Cathedral. He also continues to make English connections, directing us to the tomb of Saint Ferdinand III who took Seville from the Moors in 1248. Eleanor, the daughter of Henry II of England, was his grandmother, and the latter's husband was Alfonso VIII of Castile, and Ferdinand's daughter was Eleanor of Castile who married Edward I! He also suggests that the English supported, unsuccessfully as it turned out, Pedro the Cruel against Henry of Trastamara in their contest for the throne of Spain because John of Gaunt, the son of Edward III and the brother of the Black Prince, was married to Constance, the daughter of Pedro.

Edward, The Black Prince, was also involved in this and, according to tradition, Pedro gave him what is still called The Black Prince's Ruby which is now on the front of the English Imperial State Crown (fig. 25). It's technically not a ruby but a Spinel, although it has a small ruby mounted where there was a hole in the top of the Spinel.

It was also Pedro who was responsible for the Alcazar in Seville which Morton says "at first" he thought the most beautiful thing he'd seen in Seville, which seems to imply that he changed his mind, but I don't think he says he did; he also does say that the garden there "is the most beautiful place in Seville." The Alcazar is a Mudejar building which is essentially to say it was built by Christians, but in a style heavily influenced by Moorish decoration. Figure 26 is the Patio of the Doncellas in the Alcazar and figure 27 is the garden.

In Cordoba he was naturally very impressed by the Mezquita (Mosque)(fig. 28) which he says is "the most fantastic building of the Islamic world." In figure 29 you see the interior of the oldest part which he says reminds him of a forest full of zebras (?), and the feeling it aroused was one of delight. He recounts briefly how in the 8th century Abd al-Rahman I (remember Arabic names are transliterated in various ways) escaped Damascus when the Abbasid family overthrew his own Omayyad dynasty. He finally arrived in Cordoba and began building the mosque which was expanded by his successors. The city fell to Ferdinand III in 1236.

Morton doesn't talk about the various parts of the place, but quite a few of the more spectacular are actually Mudéjar, and even the mosaics for the Mihrab (fig. 30), the "chapel" on the side of the building in the direction of Mecca toward which prayers were made, were apparently done at least with the help of expert mosaicists sent by the Christian Eastern Emperor.

One of the most amazing Mudéjar sections is the 14th century Capilla Real (fig. 31) where Ferdinand IV and Alfonso XI are buried.

The Christian church in the middle of the mosque (see figure 28) was mostly built in the 16th c.

He made the short trip out of Cordoba to the site of the "summer palace" at Medina Azahara which he says "must have been the most splendid palace ever in Spain." The aerial view (fig. 32) was

taken more than 50 years after his visit, and by then it was much more restored than when he saw it. We're lucky that the mosque in Cordoba hasn't had to undergo anything like the amount of restoration that was required here.

His next major stop was Granada and his first memorable experience was attending a ballet performed in the gardens of the Generalife - a sort of adjunct to the Alhambra. These performances began just about the time of his visit in the late 1950's and are still going on, although in an area that is only attached to the gardens here now. The Alhambra itself was badly vandalized by the French in Napoleon's day, and some parts have had to be essentially rebuilt, and there was also extensive damage caused by a fire in 1890.

His favorite part of the place was the Courtyard of The Lions (fig.33), which has itself undergone considerable restoration recently; it gets one of only 4 color pictures in his whole book.

Surprisingly, he doesn't mention the Comares Tower, also known as the Hall of the Ambassadors. It was used as a sort of throne room and is said to have been where Columbus presented his plans to Ferdinand and Isabella immediately after they occupied Granada. In figure 34 it's at the end of the Courtyard of the Myrtles. Figure 35 is a picture of the interior.

English Morton is careful to point out that their daughter, Catherine of Aragon, was living in the Alhambra when she was betrothed to Henry VIII's older brother Arthur; after Arthur's death, as you probably know, she married Henry.

He also doesn't mention some of the more spectacular decoration like that covering the ceiling or "dome" of the Sala de Dos Hermanas (fig. 36). I've often wondered what the material is here - most sources aren't very helpful; the University of Michigan Digital Library says it's "carved and painted stucco," but I'm not sure that covers it.

In the Royal Chapel of the Cathedral of Granada he saw what he calls "the most impressive sepulchre I've ever seen," that of Ferdinand and Isabella at the left and Philip and Juana at the right (fig. 37). The Italian Domenico Fancelli made the Ferdinand and Isabella part of the sepulchre; he died before he could finish the rest, and it was completed by the Spaniard Bartolomé Ordóñez. He also saw their actual coffins (fig. 38) below the floor and called them "one of the most startling sights in Spain."

From Granada he went all the way back north to Segovia which he immediately thought "restful" and "romantic." He was naturally very impressed by the Roman aqueduct (fig. 39) which was part of a system that carried water to the city from the Rio Frio 10 miles away; it was still in use when Morton was there - and until 1973. He mentions that he ate at "a famous restaurant" near the aqueduct which must have been the Casa Candido on the right in the picture. He rarely mentions the names of restaurants where he

39

40

ate or hotels where he stayed, which seems odd.

He says that the Alcazar in Segovia (fig 40) is even more notable than the aqueduct, and it *is* a memorable building. Its history really goes all the way back to the Romans and then the Moors who had a fort there, but as it stands much of it survives from the time of Alfonso X (13th c.) The large turreted tower at the back left was erected by Juan II the father of Isabella, and she was here when she was proclaimed Queen of Castile in 1474.

The section to the right in figure 40 with the 5 spires called the "Homage" Tower is also attributed to Juan II, but Philip II apparently added the pointed roofs. Apart from the Tower of Juan II, much of the rest of the castle was rebuilt after a big fire in the 19th century. Virtually all of the interior was reconstructed and redecorated after this fire.

He also visited the little church of The True Cross (Vera Cruz) (fig. 41) just downhill from the Alcazar. Morton suggests it was built by the Templars, but apparently it was actually built by an order called The Knights of the Holy Sepulchre which still exists. According to a surviving inscription it was finished in 1208.

Nearby is the Carmelite Convent church which holds the tomb of St. John of the Cross (fig. 42) whom Morton calls "the most appealing of all Spaniards who have ever lived," and "the kindliest and sweetest of all the saints." However, he's probably most well-known today for his poem called "The Dark Night of The Soul," which is a very strange thing, and most commentaries on it seem to me to make little sense. In any case, he was certainly charismatic, as the size of his tomb ensemble and Morton's comments would indicate.

He visited Avila and calls it the highest city in Spain and the only "completely walled medieval city in Europe." That might be true at least for cities above a certain population level. Anyway, you can see how impressive it is in the picture (fig. 43). It's also a pilgrimage destination as well as a tourist focus because St. Teresa of Avila was born where the church named for her now stands, which Morton says shows "what piety can accomplish in the way of bad taste." He often fancies himself more free to evaluate architecture than painting or sculpture, about

which, as I've mentioned, he rarely says much at all.

Juan, who would have been the heir to Ferdinand and Isabella had he not died at twenty, is buried in the church of Santo Tomé in Avila. In figure 44 you can see his tomb in the foreground and the retablo behind it.

Morton points out how different European history would have been if he had lived to rule instead of Charles V, the grandson of Ferdinand and Isabella, who was then followed by Philip II. Well, yes, but that's the kind of thing that can be said about an awful lot of events in European history. What if Henry VIII's older brother Arthur hadn't died young? What if Napoleon's father had followed Pasquale Paoli and taken his family to England after the French occupied Corsica? Etc., etc.

So back through Segovia to Burgos - his route is kind of haphazard, but he doesn't comment on this. He says that the Cathedral of Burgos (fig. 45, 46) took

his breath away; after spending quite a bit of time describing it, he says, "it is not possible to describe Burgos Cathedral" - but that's just a way of saying he was very impressed - especially about its complexity and "casual magnificence."

One sculptor to whom he does devote some time is the relatively unknown Gil de Siloé who made the Retablo above the St. Anne altar which is Morton's favorite thing in this church; figure 47 is a closeup of it. Morton calls this the most beautiful carved wood he'd seen in Spain, and also one of the most charming works of sculpture, because of the way the female saints are depicted. In the picture St. Anne, the mother of Mary in the *Golden Legend*, holds her, and Mary holds the baby Jesus.

He also gives Gil de Siloé credit for the "most splendid tomb in Spain," that of Juan II of Castile and Isabel of Portugal in the Carthusian Abbey of Miraflores (fig. 48), although he'd already said the tombs in the Cathedral of Granada should have that honor.

Morton takes it for granted that Gil de Siloé was a German born in Nuremberg, but some think he was born in Orleans, and probably something like the majority of those who've studied him and his work think he was actually born in Flanders, probably Antwerp! The Nuremberg origin theory comes from Sacheverell Sitwell who also thinks he was

47

Jewish, which claim Morton says is supported by the fact that the ground plan of this tomb is in the form of an 8 pointed star - but the Star of David has 6 points, not 8!

He calls the monastery of Las Huelgas (fig. 49) in the suburbs of Burgos "the most remarkable museum of its kind in Europe," and, again, it's interesting to him partly because of another English connection: it was founded in 1170 by Eleanor, the daughter of Henry II and sister of Richard the Lion-Hearted who married Alfonso VIII in the Cathedral of Burgos, and both are buried in the choir of the church at Las Huelgas which is still a Cistercian nunnery.

48

Morton says he wanted to see their tombs (fig. 50) "as much as anything in Spain." When these and other tombs here were opened in the 1940's it was discovered that both bodies and clothing

were in much better condition than was expected, and the museum here claims that the clothing which is now on display is "the best set of medieval clothing in the world." The 13th c. silk tunic of Fernando de la Cerda who died at 19 is shown in figure 51; he was the son of Alfonso X.

Back in the city, he says that the Casa Miranda, home of the Burgos Museum, was one of the most beautiful palaces he visited in Spain. The columned courtyard is in figure 52.

In Asturias to the northwest he visited Covadonga and saw the Cave of the Virgin and the Basilica, all of which commemorates the victory of the Christian hero Pelayo near there in the 8th century which is considered the beginning of the Reconquista.

About the 30 miles to the west is Oviedo,

which doesn't seem to have impressed him very much, not even the *Camara Santa* in the Cathedral. He mentions going up in the hills to see the two "famous Gothic churches," but that's it, and they aren't Gothic at all, anyway! Santa Maria de Naranco (fig. 53) and San Miguel de Lillo (fig 54) were originally connected to the palace complex of Ramiro I of Asturias in the 9th c., and they are not even called Romanesque yet! It is said that the barrel vault in the former is the earliest

surviving example. They are also in a splendid natural setting.

On to the west he made the expected pilgrimage to Santiago de Compostela and was surprised to find that the interior was so unlike the facade. The latter is essentially 18th c.

baroque (fig. 55) (undergoing ongoing heavy repairs when this picture was taken), while the interior is mostly 12th c. Romanesque (fig. 56). He quotes the architect and critic G.E. Street who says the Portico de la Gloria (fig. 57) at the entrance to the nave is "one of the great glories of Christian art," and it does amaze Morton, but it seems to me that there are at least a few comparable examples elsewhere, especially in France, but among all of Morton's books none are devoted to France!

So back east to Leon, and he makes an observation there which is essentially what he said about the retablo in the Cathedral of Toledo - one of the chief functions of the stained glass was to "instruct the illiterate;" take a look at the stained glass in the Cathedral here and see what you learn - and you need binoculars for anything above floor level.

Salamanca, thinks Morton, might be the finest of "the glories" of Spain - "there is not a building of any age in Salamanca that is not worth looking at." That's quite a claim, but Salamanca is also one of my favorite Spanish

59

cities. He says that the "House of the Shells" (fig. 59) is one of the more "memorable" sights in the city. It was built about 1500 by a professor at the University and now houses a library.

At the University he visited the room where the poet-professor Luis de Leon gave his lectures, and he tells the story about how, after being imprisoned for a time by the Inquisition, on his return to his room he began his lecture "As I was saying…"

60

I'm surprised Morton doesn't talk more about the University; in figure 60 you can see the "plateresque" facade of one of the main buildings. Like most terms used by art historians "plateresque" is difficult - essentially impossible - to really define. You really need to look at examples of things *called* "plateresque." There are images of Ferdinand and Isabella in the circular medallion in the lower center above the doors; their son

Juan was apparently a student here when he died .Beatriz Galindo was one of the first female university students here - or anywhere - and became the Latin tutor of Queen Isabella.

The history of the two conjoined Cathedrals in Salamanca is too complicated for this commentary, and Morton doesn't talk about them at all. The New Cathedral is actually the seat of the Archdiocese, but the Old Cathedral is more interesting. The 13th c. paintings in the Chapel of St. Martin (fig. 61) here are said to be perhaps the oldest signed paintings in all of Europe - the artist was Anton de Segovia, but nothing is known about him.

The Old Cathedral also has a 16th c. organ which belonged to Francisco de Salinas who was much admired by Luis de Leon. There are many more things to see in these twin Cathedrals as well, that there isn't space to deal with here.

Figure 63 is a picture of the plateresque facade of the church of the Monastery of San Esteban in Salamanca; it's considered to be one of the finest examples of this style. Columbus is said to have stayed in the Monastery here while he was presenting his case to the geographers at the University.

The last big city Morton visited was Barcelona, and he thought Las Ramblas (fig. 64) on a summer evening among his happiest memories. However he really seems to have liked the older medieval part best, and he talks a lot about a building which he calls the Palace of the *Diputación Provincial*, but I don't know what this is. Does he mean part of what's called the Royal palace? Anyway, the latter is an interesting place, but he says absolutely nothing about all of the work of Antoni Gaudi, which is probably what most people come to Barcelona to see. This is hard to understand. Gaudi is best known as the primary architect of the Sagrada Familia (figs 65, 66), but there are many other buildings in the city of which he was the architect, and others decorated under his influence.

Morton also visited the famous monastery at Montserrat (fig 67) just northwest of Barcelona, and actually stayed in a cell there. Many come to venerate the Black Virgin, but probably many more come just out of curiosity. A lot of historically important people have made the pilgrimage here, including Charles V,

and it's where St Ignatius, in 1522, essentially made his decision to change from worldly soldier to Christian saint.

Morton says the statue of the Virgin (fig. 68) is "dark with age and the candlesmoke of centuries," but it is apparently actually *painted* black, although why this was done isn't clear. There are, in fact, many other Black Madonnas elsewhere, for whatever reason; she is rarely depicted black in paintings, and even more rarely - almost never - in the art of Western Christianity.

So off he flew to London, I guess, and maybe the final comment should be his observation that "there are few things more delightful than to have nothing to do in

a strange city with enough money to do it pleasantly!"

https://commons.wikimedia.org/wiki/File:Granada-Capilla_Real-6-Vista_general_de_los_sepulcros_de_los_Reyes_Cat%C3%B3licos.jpg

Fig. 40 Segovia Alcazar Ángel Sanz de Andrés CCBY-SA 4.0
https://en.wikipedia.org/wiki/Alc%C3%A1zar_of_Segovia#/media/File:Panor%C3%A1mica_Oto%C3%B1o_Alc%C3%A1zar_de_Segovia.jpg

Fig. 43 Avila Anual CCBY-3.0 DEED https://commons.wikimedia.org/wiki/File:Avila_001.jpg

Fig. 44 Santo Tomas Avila Selbymay CCBY-SA 3.0 ES
https://en.wikipedia.org/wiki/File:Avila_-_Convento_de_Santo_Tomas_03.jpg

Fig. 47 Burgos altar of St. Anne closeup Jl FilpoC CCBY-4.0
https://commons.wikimedia.org/wiki/File:Santa_Ana_Triple,_Gil_de_Silo%C3%A9.jpg

Fig. 48 Miraflores Jl FilpoC CCBY-SA 4.0
https://commons.wikimedia.org/wiki/File:Sepulcro_real_y_Coro_de_los_Padres,_Cartuja_de_Miraflores.jpg

Fig. 50 Las Huelgas Javi Guerra Hernando CCBY-SA 4.0 DEED
https://commons.wikimedia.org/wiki/File:Burgos-Monasterio_de_las_Huelgas-4-Tumba_de_Alfonso_VIII_y_su_esposa_Leonor_de_Plantagenet.jpg

Fig 51. Fernando de la cerda silk CCBY-SA 4.0
http://www.museodeburgos.com/index.php?option=com_content&task=section&id=16&Itemid=149#

Fig. 52 Burgos Casa Miranda   Jose Luis Filpo Cabana CCBY-3.0 DEED
https://commons.wikimedia.org/wiki/File:Casa_de_Miranda,_Burgos._Patio.jpg

Fig. 58 Leon   Jcfll 44 CCBY-SA 4.0 DEED
https://commons.wikimedia.org/wiki/File:Wideview_of_windows_Of_Le%C3%B3n_Cathedral.jpg

Fig. 64 Las Ramblas Banja-Frans Mulder CCBY 3.0 DEED
https://commons.wikimedia.org/wiki/File:Spain_-Barcelona,_La_Rambla_-_panoramio_%281%29.jpg

Fig. 68. Black Madonna   Csiraf CCBY-SA 3.0 DEED
https://upload.wikimedia.org/wikipedia/commons/thumb/3/30/Black_Madonna.jpg/682px-Black_Madonna.jpg

A COMMENTARY ON *THE WANING OF THE MIDDLE AGES* BY JOHAN HUIZINGA

The Late Jan Huizinga was a professor at the University of Leiden and is today probably the most widely known Dutch historian, having written several books on what can be called "the history of civilization" or "cultural history.". The first English translation of *The Waning of the Middle Ages* was by Frits Hopman, an associate of Huizinga's whom the latter praises highly for his rendering of the Dutch into English. This is the translation one reads in the 1954 Anchor Books edition. Since then there have been two more translations, changing the book's title for starters, to *The Autumn of The Middle Ages* (1996) and *The Autumntide of the Middle Ages* (2020). The editors of these later editions are, of course, strongly critical of Hopman with whom Huizinga himself, who was fluent in English, seemed completely satisfied.

So what's good enough for Huizinga is good enough for me, and, in any case, it's Hopman's translation with which I'm familiar - and, by the way, exactly what language does "Autumntide" come from? It's not in your *English* dictionary.

One other thing I should say here though, is that the *Autumntide* translation has color pictures, and that gives it one important advantage over the old Anchor version which has no pictures at all.

Willem Otterspeer who has written a book about Huizinga called *Reading Huizinga* in which he is on the whole very sympathetic, says that "those who read him as an historian will scarcely discover any cohesiveness in his work" And apropos of that, I do think it is often difficult in reading the book to see the forest for the trees. It's almost more like a collection of essays than a succession of chapters with a common theme - and at least one of the chapters *has* been excerpted and included in a collection of essays. In *this* essay, therefore, I'm going to be less concerned with the overall program, and more concerned with various individual points he makes, sometimes random things he says, and interesting issues which he brings up.

The very first sentence in the book is, for example, an odd one; he says "History has always been more engrossed by problems of origins than by those of decline and fall." But what does that remind you of? Perhaps the most famous work of history ever written, Gibbon's The *Decline and Fall of The Roman Empire.* The work of most historians is, I think, easier to describe as focused essentially on just telling us what happened, and maybe why. Also, I think it would be hard to defend his claim that " in medieval history we (historians) have been searching so diligently for the origins of modern culture" that we tend to see the Middle Ages as little more than a prelude to the Renaissance." But what's "modern culture?" Is Voltaire part of it? Beethoven? Picasso? Do any historians try to put the "origins" of these fellows in the Middle Ages?

He says that the idea of writing a book that "deals with the history of the fourteenth and fifteenth centuries regarded as . . . the close of the Middle Ages presented itself to him while he was "endeavoring to arrive a a genuine understanding of the art of the Van Eyck brothers and their contemporaries . . . in connection with the entire life of their times." That's OK, but Jan Van Eyck's brother Hubert is a very shadowy figure, and there is really very little, if anything, that can be attributed to him with certainty.

My main problem with his treatment of the "Van Eyck brothers" is that he insists they aren't Renaissance painters. He claims that art historians "have confounded, very wrongly, realism and Renaissance." So compare Van Eyck's work (fig. 1)with that of Hans Holbein whom no one calls "medieval" (fig.2), and the anonymous artist who did the surviving 9th c. work in the church of St. Johann in Müstair in Switzerland (fig. 3). Which is more like Van Eyck's painting? It is a little difficult to make such comparisons, because there are not many panel paintings as early as the 9th c., or even the 13th. However, figure 4 is a picture of a fresco by Fra Angelico who was Van Eyck's contemporary, and I think the same point about realism can be made. I'd be the last to claim that terms like "medieval" and "Renaissance" are easy to define; I'm just appealing here to how art historians use language. Some manuscript decoration done in the Middle Ages, especially in Anglo-Saxon England is certainly done with incredible attention to detail, but it is not "realistic." Figure 5 is a closeup of a page from the *Book of Kells* c. 800.

In Janson's standard *History of Art* the sources for Part II, The Middle Ages, end in 1300 and Van Eyck is discussed in Part Three called "The Renaissance Through The Rococo." In Marilyn Stokstad's *Art History*, another standard text now,

Van Eyck is discussed under "Humanism and the Northern Renaissance," and she mention's that "the desire for an accurate depiction of the world" was characteristic of the period.

Another important thing Huizinga says right at the start, although it's not original, is that most of us take a awful lot for granted, and that it's hard for us to imagine "the keenness with which a fur coat, a good fire on the hearth . . . were formerly enjoyed." The essay in this book called "The Road Behind" is relevant to this point.

The first chapter is called "The Violent Tenor of Life," and in it he says that "A present day reader studying the history of the Middle Ages based on official documents will never sufficiently realize the extreme excitability of the medieval soul." But then he says these documents are our "most reliable sources." This looks close to self-contradiction. Instead of using these sources then, whatever their status, he uses a lot of anecdotes which do make for memorable reading, but I doubt they are really necessary to convince most of us that it wouldn't be a good idea to trade most of 2024 America for most of 1024 Europe. He wrote this book in 1924 so he must remember the "violent tenor" of life in his own day, and he was to live on through the most violent period in the whole history of the planet. How much violence and "excitability" people are exposed to in a given age is hard to generalize about; a lot just depends on random time and place - if you lived in California from 1900 to 1960 you were a lot luckier than those who lived through that period in much of Europe.

To illustrate the character of medieval violence he focuses on Philip the Good, Duke of Burgundy and his desire for revenge on the French royal family because his father, John the Fearless, was assassinated with the approval of the king's son, the future Charles VII. Again and again Huizinga emphasizes the significance of revenge as a medieval motive. Well, suppose someone kills your father today - are you going to be inclined to forgive and forget, or do you want the killer punished? That is, do you want revenge?

He says, putting it a little strongly I think, that "the Middle Ages knew nothing of . . . our sentiment of justice," with our "doubts as to the criminal's responsibility; the conviction that society is, to a certain extent, the accomplice of the individual; the desire to reform instead of inflicting pain . . ." etc. Even if our legal systems today are more "just," trying to quantify "society's" part in a crime is, of course, very difficult, and I suppose everyone is in favor of reforming criminals, but a lot of murderers only want to kill one person; after that, they are no longer a danger to society, and are then, in a manner of speaking, "reformed." But should they be allowed to go free, even if, *per impossibile*, we could know they would be fine citizens henceforth? Do they, as it were, get a free one? Just for the record, about 30% of those who have committed violent crimes and are released, wind up in prison again, having committed more violent crimes.

And with regard to the conflicts involving Philip the Good and the French, they all took place in the 15th century, and the most well-known portraits of Philip the Good (fig 6) and his son Charles the Bold were painted by Van der Weyden who, like Van Eyck, is never called a medieval painter now. The most well-known portrait of Charles VII (not shown) is by Jean Fouquet who, like Van der Weyden, is covered in the "Renaissance to Rococo" part of Janson's history, and they are both likewise covered in the same section of Stokstad's book which I mentioned earlier. For comparison, figure 7 is a medieval (13th century) portrait of Louis IX. The jury is, again, against Huizinga.

Much later in the book he also briefly discusses another legal issue, and says that what he calls the "formalism" of "primitive law" which knew "no difference between the intentional and the involuntary deed" was something from which jurisprudence had been freed at the close of the Middle Ages. This is another pretty grand generalization. In any case, we have here an issue which still inspires arguments today. If I intentionally run a stop sign and accidentally kill someone, should I just get a ticket, or be charged with felony involuntary manslaughter? If I didn't intend to kill someone, should I be punished for bad luck? What if I intend to kill someone but forget to load my pistol so that when I pull the trigger it just goes click click? Should I avoid the gas chamber just because I was lucky? With a good lawyer I'd probably do no time at all, even though I fully intended to kill someone.

Huizing claims that "in general" the idea works of art give us of an epoch " is far more serene and happy than that which we glean in reading its chronicles, documents, or even literature." This is a hard theory to evaluate. For one thing, he suggests that "a man of culture" today, if asked to characterize 15th c. French civilization would refer to Van Eyck, Van der Weyden, *inter alia*, but these artists aren't even French! I doubt even "a man of culture," would be able to name more than one or two 15th century French chronicles of any sort; try it yourself. Time's up. If you get into another "epoch," like the 16th c., some of the most well known paintings are not at all easy to describe as "serene and happy" - there's Bosch's work, some of which is actually 15th c., and Grunewald's Isenheim Altarpiece to name two famous things "a man of culture" would probably know about. I suppose one could call Montaigne's essays "serene"and Shakespeare's comedies "happy" in that century, but this is, again, a hard thing to evaluate.

Another claim he makes which is difficult to make sense of is that "in an epoch of pre-eminently visual inspiration like the fifteenth century pictorial expression easily surpasses literary expression." To start with, this looks like a tautology, but, anyway, what does "surpasses" mean here? What counts as evidence? How do you compare Van Eyck's *Giovanni Arnolfini and His Bride* to Mallory's King Arthur epic *Le Morte d'Arthur*, or the poetry of Villon, or Boiardo's *Orlando*, or Pico della Mirandola's *On the Dignity of Man*?

Huizinga says that "to the medieval spirit, musical emotion quite naturally took the form of an echo of celestial joy," and "the ecstatic character of musical emotion . . . did not escape them." I think, based on this kind of talk, that he would agree that music is the most powerful artform - compare what happens at a Rolling Stones concert to the crowd's behavior at, say, a Jasper Johns exhibit if you want evidence for that claim.

Huizinga himself says that "ill considered generalization . . . manifests itself on every page of the literature of the time . . . ." *Every* page? Some might call that an ill-considered generalization, though one not as philosophically significant as his comments comparing painting and literature.

It's interesting that most of the faults he finds in the era which his book covers are not ones he attributes specifically to the visual arts. The age, he says, "seems to us to display an incredible superficiality and feebleness. The complexity of things is ignored in a truly astounding manner." Furthermore, "inexactness, credulity . . . inconstancy, are common features of medieval reasoning . . . ." Works of art can, of course, also mislead; Rubens' paintings extolling the virtues of Marie de Medici come to mind, but the most celebrated paintings of the 15th c., as Huizinga points out, have religious subjects, and one might argue that a work of art like, say, the *Ghent Altarpiece* isn't open to the same *kind* of evaluation as a secular work of art - although the way in which Christian heroes are represented in paintings can certainly be criticized. A lot could be said here about this kind of thing, but this is a short essay, not a doctoral dissertation

In conclusion, I'd just say that, for me, the book is most valuable as a source of anecdotes and interesting quotations which I might never have run across if I had not read it. It's less valuable for the author's theories. The difference between the Middle Ages and the Renaissance is not as clear as the difference in taste between a strawberry and an apple, despite what he says.

THE ROAD BEHIND: A COMMENTARY ON *THE DISCOVERERS* BY DANIEL BOORSTIN

Bill Gates' Bestseller *The Road Ahead* is both an interesting more or less autobiographical account of the history of Microsoft as well as a modest attempt to predict some relatively short term advances along the information highway - or super-highway - most of which have been achieved by the time I'm writing this - 2023, about 25 years after the book was published. What would be really interesting is to have some at least defensible predictions about what things along this highway will be like a hundred or a thousand years or more in the future, but few have had any success, except of course in the most general and uninteresting way, at predicting the future about anything.

I think Daniel Boorstin's book *The Discoverers* might, conversely, be called *The Road Behind.* Instead of dealing with what might happen in the future, he's writing about what has happened in the past, and most of us know as little about that subject as we do about the future. We take for granted the amazing things that have been discovered and invented which have led to Microsoft and the information superhighway that started out as a dirt path in the wilderness - and some of these discoveries seem to have been more like the occurrence of a miracle than like discoveries or inventions as we usually use those words. I've written elsewhere about the seemingly miraculous discovery of a method by which fire could be made ("We Have Ignition" in *Pencils Out*, volume II). The discovery of how to make fire is an example of an all or nothing sort of event - you either get fire by, for example, rubbing sticks together in some way, or banging rocks together, or whatever other incredible method was discovered, or you don't.

Most "inventions" or "discoveries" are however a product of gradual development. The discovery of how to live a settled life, create a community, a village etc. - the event called the Neolithic Revolution - is an example of this, and., of course, this revolution had to take place before most other discoverers could make their contributions. The usual view is that the transition from hunting and gathering to farming and ranching began around 12000 years ago in Mesopotamia and perhaps somewhat later in other independent locations around the world. As an aside, it does have to be considered a little surprising that this revolution happened in places as far away and as apparently independent of one another as China and Mexico within a few thousand years. That may seem like a long time, but in archaeological time it's not that much, considering that homo sapiens has been around at least 100,000 years

Unlike the various kinds of evidence that allow archaeologists to date the development of settled life, the chronology of the development of the use of language is much harder to establish. It is thought that, anatomically, humans had the ability to make essentially all modern vocal sounds to allow them to have a language like those around today by at least 50,000 B.C. based on skeletal remains. But from grunts and howls to anything like a real language one would imagine to have taken a long time. However it is possible that some nameless fellow did reasonably systematize these kinds of sounds into, I suppose, something like Cro-Magnonese.

Although many advances in things like farming, building, and so on could be passed down orally once there was a reasonably useful language, to progress much farther required not only language, but *written* language which could effectively provide the kind of sophisticated help which one generation could use to build on the work of another, and the usual view is that, while there is some evidence for the use of symbols to identify animals etc., for example, from European sources as early as 35000 B.C. the origin of what can reasonably be called written language is usually assigned to 4th millennium B.C. Mesopotamia, and somewhat later to China, India, and Mesoamerica.

Although *some* earlier languages were to *some* extent phonetic, the next big jump was to the essentially completely phonetic alphabets of the Phoenicians, Greeks, and Romans, the Latin alphabet of the latter having proven to be one of the most significant contributions of the ancient world, and now in use from one end of this world to the other.

Boorstin only really begins his treatment of significant discoveries at about this point, and the first thing to which he devotes a lot of pages is the development of clocks and calendars. The Egyptians used what's called the heliacal rising of Sirius - the occasion on which the especially bright star Sirius appears directly opposite the rising sun, as their New Year's Day. They divided the year into 12 30 day months with an added 5 day festival for a total of 365 days. Julius Caesar took this arrangement to Europe, whence it became known as the Julian Calendar, and it was in general use until the 16th century - and beyond in some places - when the so-called Gregorian Calendar which adds an extra day every "leap year" and is still in use today, was adopted.

Although the date for the writing of *Genesis* is still debated, virtually all agree that it was essentially complete as we have it by no later than the 5th century B.C., well before the Romans began using a 7 day week, the idea for which may have come somehow from

Judaism, odd as this might seem. The 7 day week was, however, apparently common in the Near East while the Romans were still using an 8 day week; in any case Constantine decreed that the 7 day week was official Roman use as of 321.

All this began with the recognition of the heliacal rising of Sirius, and this must have been, like the discovery of how to make fire, the result of an observation by one man, although we have, of course, no idea who he was. This observation-discovery was not the product of a gradual development like the settled villages of the Neolithic Revolution, or the development of written language, although these, too, were likely the products of the decisions and cleverness of just a few men.

The name of the first fellow to argue that the earth is round isn't known, but by the time Plato's *Phaedo* was written it was taken for granted in at least some quarters, counter-intuitive though it must have seemed. We do, however, know the name of the first fellow to discover a way to accurately measure the Earth's circumference - Eratosthenes of Cyrene in the early 2nd century B.C. Again, this was *essentially* an all or nothing discovery, although he did, as head of the Library of Alexandria, have access to a lot of research by others.

Boorstin spends a lot of time talking about the exploration of this round world in a very interesting way, and it's obvious that Columbus, Vasco da Gama, and Magellan, should be considered among those amazing individuals who at least set off the developments that followed. Each made a discovery that would change the lives of millions of people in the future - although the Vikings had made temporary settlements in North America, it was Columbus who really made the difference, da Gama discovered the route to the East around Africa, and Magellan discovered how to get to the East by sailing west.

By the time these sea voyages were being made, the very important magnetic compass had been in use for some time, but I guess we just have to suppose that some unnamed person figured out that rubbing a needle on a lodestone and suspending it by a thread or putting it on a piece of cork to float in bowl, would result in its pointing north. Boorstin himself suggests that one person was, in effect, the inventor of the compass, we just don't know who he was. This essentially all or nothing discovery may have first been made in China, but it may be that it was made independently elsewhere; in any case it was in its European employment that its full potential was realized.

Boorstin says that "the leap from naked eye observation to instrument aided vision would be one of the great advances in the history of the planet." Instrument aided vision involves primarily the use of 3 distinct devices - the telescope, the microscope, and eyeglasses. It may be that all three were, in effect, Dutch inventions. According to Boorstin the telescope should probably be credited to Hans Lippershey and the microscope to Zacharias Jansen both about 1608. Both of these fellows lived in the small town of Middelburg in southwestern Holland near the border with Belgium, and, amazingly, they were even next door neighbors for a while and did not get along well. In any case it was not long before great advances were made in the use of these things by inventors and discoverers like Galileo and Van Leeuwenhoek.

In this essay I'm more or less trying to point out the things that have really changed our lives, and the telescope, interesting as it is, and although it does have practical earthbound uses, pretty much only changes the lives of astronomers. The microscope on the other hand obviously became an invaluable medical tool that has changed, in one way or another, almost all our lives insofar as we have access to doctors and hospitals. I think one could claim, however, that eyeglasses have made an even more overall impact. Both Lippershey and Jansen apparently made eyeglasses, but the technique had already been around for hundreds of years and to whom we should give ultimate credit isn't known. Eyeglasses themselves were essentially just an improvement on the various kinds of handheld magnifiers that had been known since antiquity.

To some extent the capacity to print books - 9,000,000 in the second half of the 15th century alone, according to the Britannica - is a "development" but Johann Gutenberg is always given credit for the real breakthrough. To do his work, however, he needed the screw press which had been around since the Romans were apparently the first inventors thereof, and he needed paper, the invention of which is usually credited to the Chinese, although various sorts of writing material, mostly made from papyrus or animal hyde (parchment) had been around in the Mediterranean world since antiquity. By the late Middle Ages, however, the technique for making what we think of as paper was widespread in Europe. He also needed an appropriate kind of oil based ink which he himself is given credit for inventing.

The simple Latin alphabet, unlike the very complicated eastern writing systems, was crucial to his project, along with the use of movable type. For 500 years his invention was to be the main vehicle for the dissemination of knowledge - as well as ignorance.

Mathematics, says Boorstin, is the Latin of the scientific world. One of the crucial events in its history was the invention of what's called the Arabic number system, which is actually an Indian invention. If you don't think the Arabic system has an advantage over Roman numerals, try doing your income tax with the latter next time. We have no idea to whom we should give credit for originating the Arabic system, but it was in use in parts of Europe as early as the 10th century. Although, surprisingly, Boorstin doesn't talk about them, Gerbert of Aurillac who became Pope Sylvester I, and Leonardo of Pisa also known as Fibonacci, are usually the ones given credit for popularizing it. Another big "invention" in the field of mathematics was the decimal system for which the Dutchman Simon Stevin (16th century) is given credit, and which many of us use almost as often as we use Arabic numbers.

Boorstin doesn't give as much attention to Newton and Leibniz as might be expected, but as one might also say of Galileo, their discoveries were not such as to affect the lives of most of us. The exception might be the invention of calculus for which both Newton and Leibniz claimed credit, though there are precedents of a sort well back in the history of mathematics. Without going into detail, I will just quote John von Neumann who says that "it would be difficult to overestimate its importance" in a lot of areas that do affect our lives - computer science, medicine, physics and engineering, chemistry, etc.

Einstein's Theory of General Relativity was expressed using calculus, and he is said to have had the pictures of 2 English scientists on the wall of his study - Newton and Michael Faraday and the latter, along with James Clerk Maxwell, who used calculus in his seminal *Treatise on Electricity and Magnetism*, should get a lot of credit for beginning the progress toward all the sorts of conveniences of modern life made possible by the generation of electricity.

It's essentially with Faraday and Maxwell that Boorstin ends his book, and he does not go on into the world of Edison, Watt, the Wright brothers, Henry Ford, let alone those who came along after *The Discoverers* was written and whose work led to the capacity we now have to put over 200,000 books and about as many audio books along with virtually every significant or popular piece of music ever written in our pockets! *Gratias ago*!

Made in the USA
Las Vegas, NV
01 February 2024

85184614R00079